Fiorello La Guardia

Fiorello La Guardia

by BELLA RODMAN
in collaboration with Philip Sterling

HILL AND WANG · NEW YORK

Manufactured in the United States of America
by The Colonial Press Inc., Clinton, Massachusetts

To My Son

ACKNOWLEDGMENTS

I should like to express my indebtedness to the many people who, by their own enthusiasm and eagerness to see a biography of La Guardia written, contributed in no small measure to this work. I am especially grateful to Ellen Lewis Buell, Children's Book Editor of *The New York Times* and Lecturer in English at Columbia University School of General Studies. Her encouragement and assistance came at a time when it was most needed. Frank Giordano, the charming alter ego of Fiorello La Guardia, was the source of valuable insights into the character of the man he idolized. And Gemma La Guardia Gluck, Fiorello's sister, has been unstinting in sharing her family reminiscences with me.

Lorine W. Garrett, of Sharlot Hall Historical Society Museum of Arizona; James Katsaros, Administrator of the Municipal Archives and Records of New York City; and Shirley Abrams, Librarian, Special Projects, CBS News, have been most generous with their help.

I also wish to thank the following individuals who were kind enough to share important firsthand knowledge of Fiorello La Guardia with me:

Harry G. Andrews and Louis Espresso, his earliest teachers in the art of practical politics; A. A. Berle, Jr., former New Deal Brain Truster, now Professor of Corporation Law at Columbia University Law School; George F. Briegel, Bandmaster of the New York City Fire Department, 1921-58; Eugene R. Canudo, La Guardia's secretary in Congress, 1931-33, elected Chairman of the La Guardia Memorial Association in 1961; Dr. Vincent Caso, City Hall reporter since 1919; Edward Corsi, Director of Emergency Home Relief Bureau, 1934-35, and Deputy Commissioner of Welfare, 1935-40; Mrs. Carrie Curcio, who made the acquaintance of the young La Guardia when they were both working at Ellis Island; Nathan Frankel, Labor Secretary to Mayor La Guardia, 1937-40; the late Stanley M. Isaacs, Borough President of Manhattan, 1938-41, Republican minority leader of the City Council; and finally, Lowell Limpus, of the New York *Daily News*, friend and early biographer of the Little Flower.

BELLA RODMAN

CONTENTS

LIST OF ILLUSTRATIONS

Plates start facing page 119

The author and the publisher hereby acknowledge the sources
of the illustrations appearing in this book:
Brown Brothers—Plates 2, 10, 16, 18; United Press International—4, 5, 7-9, 11-13, 15, 19; Acme—6, 17; Wide World Photos
—14, 20, 26; Sharlot Hall Historical Museum of Arizona—1; Italian
Dressmakers Local 89 ILGWU—3.

CHAPTER 1

Hard Times

PAPA LOOKED LIKE A STRANGER WHEN HE CAME HOME that cold April evening in 1885. He still had his cornet under his arm, leather case and all, but his brown coat with the black velvet collar was gone. So was his brown derby hat. Instead, he was wearing a uniform.

Mama Irene said good evening without looking up from the stove but when she turned and saw him, she exclaimed, "Achille! You have joined a band."

Achille smiled. He executed a military rightabout-face and then another one so that his wife could inspect him from every angle. "I have not only joined a band," he said proudly, "I have joined the United States Army and I am wearing its uniform. I am no longer a mere cornet virtuoso, I am a Chief Musician, a *maestro*, the leader of the band."

"Achille," said Irene, "*tu sei magnifico*."

"*Vero, vero*," he laughed. Then he turned to the children. "Fiorello, Gemmina. How do I look? What do you think of your papa?"

Fiorello, round and tough as a rubber doll, bounded into his father's arms. The little two-and-a-half-year-old excitedly fingered the brass buttons, the gold braid, the regimental insignia. Gemma, a year older, came close and looked on quietly. To both of them, though they didn't know the word, their father looked truly magnificent. The uniform gave a new splendor to his neatly trimmed black beard and mustache, his swarthy complexion, his short stalwart frame.

It was for the children and his chestnut-haired, brown-eyed wife that Achille had joined the Army. Enlistment meant an end to worrying where his next job was coming from, how long it would last, how much it would pay. It meant an escape from the crowding, dirt, and disorder in this new immigrant neighborhood.

When Achille visited the United States for the first time in 1878 as musical arranger and accompanist for the famous Italian soprano, Adelina Patti, his spirit expanded at the sight of the country's vastness and freedom. Surely an able musician who spoke four languages and had traveled all over Europe and the Dutch East Indies could do well in America. That was why Achille, at thirty-one, went back to his native Italy to find a bride. Irene and he were married in Trieste on June 3, 1880.

With the ink still wet on their marriage certificate the couple sailed for New York and rented a tight little two-room tenement flat at 7 Varick Street in Greenwich Village. Gemma was born there on April 24, 1881, and Fiorello on December 11, 1882. But during the five years since their arrival, the La Guardias' dream of a prosperous life in the New World had kept its distance, pursue it as they would.

Achille was becoming just another musician who spent more time looking for work than working. The truth was that times were hard and getting harder. Irene learned English as quickly as she could to please her husband, who was so in love with their new country that he wanted their children to grow up, from the cradle, as "real Americans." But there were frightening words in this new language: "panic," "unemployment," "eviction." She discovered that "hunger" was what you felt before suppertime. "Starvation" was what your family would face if you did not have a "job." That word, "job," was all-important. The immigrants had even turned it into an Italian word, *giobba*. Irene studied the meaning of this grim vocabulary in the faces of men and women in her own neighborhood. She heard echoes of those words in her own unspoken anxieties.

Fiorello and Gemma were still admiring their papa. He was showing them how a Chief Musician conducts a U. S. Army band. Irene permitted herself to enjoy the spectacle for a moment. Then she cried, "Achille, children, enough! Supper is on the table."

As they sat, Irene surveyed her family. This Achille was a man of strength and spirit. A defiant man, who had run away from home in Foggia during his early teens because he resented the harsh discipline of the church school he attended. A rebellious man, who had written on his marriage certificate, under the head of religion, "*nessuna*"—nothing. A humane man, who fiercely rejected the oppressive European structure of king and commoner, peasant and *padrone*, but who thrilled to the democratic mood of America. A warm man with a ready laugh and a quick temper, who loved his family with Italian intensity. This was the man, baptized in the Catholic faith as Achille Luigi Carlo La Guardia, for whom she had gladly gone to the uncertainties of a new life in a new land.

Gemma, the first-born, looked and behaved as a four-year-old might. She was placid, inclined to wait for things to happen. But not Fiorello. Placidity was not in him. At two-and-a-half, his hair still in long ringlets, he was no longer a baby. At play with Gemma, he seized the leadership when he could. His restlessness showed even at the table, where he ate eagerly and efficiently.

The night after Achille's enlistment was a night of celebration and farewell spent with friends who came to the La Guardia flat. The coal-burning kitchen stove was well stoked. There was Italian bread, red wine, and pale yellow *provalone* cheese on the table. And there was talk, the talk of immigrants considering their lives, recollecting their common past, and speculating about their future. Fiorello was far too young to understand the words or the ideas. But the voices around him rang with an intensity which commanded his attention and made him eager to grasp the meanings behind the earnest talk of the grownups.

"We will have to leave New York and go with the regiment," Achille told his friends, "perhaps even to the Far West. Soon, I hope. It will be good for the children. They will grow up as real *Americani*."

One of the visitors agreed wistfully. "Maybe it will be better for all of you. Here in New York, things are bad. Everyone talks only about jobs, jobs, but so many men are without work."

"Yes," said another. "This *miseria* has fallen on all the working people. Those who have jobs live in fear of losing them. The jobless must live on their faith, their hope, and on the charity of those who can give them a handful of *pasta* or a bucket of coal."

"*Vero*," sighed a third man. "Today, I saw many women standing in the cold at the door of Trinity Church, where the rich Protestants go. They were waiting with empty buckets for coal. Some did not get any because there was not enough. All of the charity offices closed their doors early because there was no more food to distribute."

Everyone had ideas, everyone spoke up. Perhaps President Cleveland, who confronted the trusts and the monopolies so boldly, would find a solution.

"He is a *politicante* like all the rest," said one of the guests. "Politicians promise, but they do not do. They take, but they do not give. Don't we see the face of Tammany Hall right here on Varick Street? True, the Irish politician with the big cigar has given away many fifty-cent pieces, but only to those who promise to vote for the candidates of Tammany in November."

"Make it easier for poor people to get free land in the West," someone suggested. "In the city, without land of his own, a man cannot work for himself. He can only sell his strength and his skill to others—if there is work for him to do."

"Isn't it true," someone else asked, "that there would be more jobs if there were a shorter working day? Today, those who have jobs work twelve, fourteen, fifteen hours a day. But if there were an eight-hour day for everyone . . ."

"The time will come," Achille interrupted. Pointing to his son, he smiled, "Fiorello and his friends will live to see it, and so will many of us."

One of the men shrugged; another dissented loudly.

Achille persisted. "America will live through this panic as it did through the panic of 1873. I have faith in America."

The bread, the wine, and the cheese had slowly disappeared. Despite the earnest talk, the mood grew less somber. "Enough," cried a guest. "This is a celebration. Listen!" And he sang a Calabrian song. Other songs followed the first, sad ones, merry ones, songs of Naples, tunes from the mountains of Abruzzi, farmers' songs and fishermen's songs, until Achille said, "Amici, here is an American song. In the big cities, many people are singing it these days:

> 'We want to feel the sunshine,
> We want to smell the flowers.
> We're sure that God has willed it
> And we mean to have eight hours!' "

Two Armies

FROM THE TIME HE WAS THREE, FIORELLO AND HIS family felt the sunshine and smelled the flowers of a dozen states west of the Hudson River. There were biting winters and blazing summers at Fort Sully, North Dakota. All he ever remembered of that first venture beyond Manhattan's pavements was a prairie fire and the birth of his brother, Richard, in June, 1887. There was more of winter and summer, of growing up and of trying the world on for size at Sackets Harbor, New York, on the eastern edge of Lake Ontario's blue-green sweep to the Canadian horizon.

In 1890, Achille and Irene packed pots and pans, bedding, and musical instruments for a third time. By railroad and six-mule Army wagon, they made a long two-thousand-mile jump to Fort Huachuca, in the Arizona Territory. Fiorello, eight years old, was grown-up enough to have responsibilities on the wearisome journey. He rode herd on Gemma's violin, Richard's drum, and his own cornet, while Gemma carried Mama's bandbox full of bonnets and helped keep Richard dry and happy. Papa, naturally, was trail boss of the whole La Guardia outfit. He maintained discipline and morale and told them what he knew about the unfamiliar American landscapes through which they passed and the heroes and villains that once lived there:

7

"Papa, I don't see any buffaloes out here. I thought there would be lots of buffaloes."

"There used to be."

"Then where are they now?"

"Buffalo Bill and his hunters slaughtered them to feed the workers who made the railroad."

"Where is Buffalo Bill now?"

"He is an actor in a Wild West show."

"Did Buffalo Bill kill Indians, too?"

"Everybody killed Indians."

Huachuca was a dry mudhole of an Army stockade fifteen miles north of the Mexican border and forty miles from anywhere else. The original owners of the country, Apache, Papago, Navajo, Maricopa, Yavapai, Hualpai, and Havasupai, were still around but they were no longer warlike. Cochise, wise and fearless defender of his people, was a long time dead. Geronimo, last of the great Apache warriors, was alive, in a military prison at Fort Sill, Oklahoma. White scalps were safe. The Indians' dream of recapturing independence on the land of their forefathers had become history.

The La Guardias moved their belongings into a two-room adobe house with a canvas-roofed outdoor kitchen in the area where officers and privileged noncoms lived with their families. Because there was always family wash flapping on clotheslines behind the houses, the enlisted men called the street "Soapsuds Row."

To an eight-year-old boy, Arizona was a playground without a fence. There were burros to ride, kangaroo rats to chase, and real guns to shoot (under adult supervision). When a boy was alone, he could walk through long empty stretches pretending he was a prospector, an Indian scout, or General Garibaldi leading his army into Naples.

Fort Huachuca, however, didn't have much to offer to most adults except a living. In the case of the La Guardias this meant Achille's Army pay, free rent, and the hope that they could move to a bigger Army post. They did, two years later.

Whipple Barracks, population two thousand, was less than a

mile from Prescott on a mile-high plateau in central Arizona. The town was laid out around a spacious plaza, with the streets crossing each other at right angles, and was encircled by hills. A bandstand graced the plaza's center and the perimeter was lined with commercial buildings and stores that served the townspeople and the folk of the far-flung countryside. There was a sawmill, a brick yard, and a red brick school house more elegant than any Fiorello had ever attended.

For the La Guardias this was a return to civilization. The Army gave them a very respectable five-room house with a lean-to kitchen. In the roomy parlor they set up the organ, laid a green-and-rose-flowered carpet on the floor, and hung a large ornate oil lamp with crystal pendants from the ceiling. They kept rabbits, chickens and, later, three cows.

Fiorello was assigned to the job of selling milk to other families on the post. Irene did the cooking all year round, but at Christmas it was Chief Musician La Guardia who went into the kitchen to become head cook for the year's most important feast. Naturally, Fiorello helped whenever he could. He learned to make excellent spaghetti sauces.

There were music lessons in the parlor and Papa, who wasn't strict with the children ordinarily, became a stern bandmaster, demanding as much from Gemma and Fiorello as he did from the soldiers of his Eleventh Infantry Band. He would sit at the organ, play a few bars, and then snap, "Let's hear it! Quick now! Without a mistake!" A good try wasn't good enough; the children had to do it correctly. Achille promised that when they were proficient enough, they could join his young people's club in Prescott, where he earned extra money by giving music lessons.

Young Fiorello did not think highly of school. The hours dragged, the lessons were dull, and his mind was elsewhere. His teacher told Bandmaster La Guardia on the street one day, "Your son is a bright boy but he is too inattentive."

When Mama heard the reports, she chided Fiorello. "Why can't you sit still and pay attention? A restless boy will never be a learned man."

What Fiorello was really interested in lay in the world outside his classroom. He was looking for answers to questions which had troubled him even while he was at Huachuca. Why, for instance, did the officers' children treat him so oddly? Sometimes they were friendly, other times they behaved as if he didn't exist. Was it because he was so short for his age? Was it because his father was an "*Eye*-talian"? Maybe it was because his father was just a Chief Musician instead of a commissioned officer? Or was it all of these put together?

These were tough questions for a youngster to settle, or to ask of his parents. He was beginning to understand, however, that there was some kind of a pattern in which people lived with each other. He could feel the pattern, but it was more important to understand it. When he came to Prescott, he was ten years old. He wanted to know where he fitted in.

One hint came from Matt, the tall red-headed boy at school who yelled at Fiorello now and again: "The night goes out and the *Dagos* in!"

Another time, an Italian organ-grinder with a monkey came to town. The children gathered around to hear the tinkly music and watch the bright-eyed little animal in its red Zouave jacket. When you handed it a penny it would snatch the coin and tip its tiny red hat. Fiorello's schoolmates kept hollering, "A Dago with a monkey" and a few of them said, "Hey, Fiorello, you're a Dago, too. Where's your monkey?" These insults hurt. To make matters worse, Papa came along, talked loudly and cordially with the organ-grinder, and invited him home to dinner.

Fiorello discovered Item One in the pattern. If you were short and funny-looking, if your parents were born in a foreign country and spoke English with an accent, the other kids considered themselves superior to you. They could call you insulting names. So it seemed that people were separated according to place of birth, native American on one side, foreign born on the other.

Of course, Matt chanted "the night goes out and the Dagos in" once too often. Fiorello charged like an infuriated ram, butted him in the belly, and ran out of reach while Matt gasped for breath. Pattern or no, Mrs. La Guardia's shrill-voiced little boy was not one to be pushed around. He got into fights often. Joey

Bauer would lick him almost every day, but Fiorello came back for more. The story goes that once, outdoors, when he was fighting a schoolmate who was much taller than he was, Fiorello took time out and ran into the building and came back with a chair to stand on so he could swing at his opponent's face.

Another Item. Papa and Mama were both born in Italy, but they didn't have the same religion. When they were living in Sackets Harbor Mama told him and Gemma that she was Jewish. Mama's mother was Fiorina Luzzato, whose family had lived in Trieste for almost three hundred years. Fiorello was named for her. Her first name meant "little flower" in Italian. Mama's father was Abramo Isacco Coen, whose family had lived in Spalato, in what is now Yugoslavia, for at least a century.

True, he and Gemma went to the Episcopal Sunday School, but Mama was a Jew just the same. The Mexicans who worked on the railroad were neither Jews nor Episcopalians—they were Catholics. The Chinese who ran most of the restaurants in town —they had some religion of their own.

That was Item Two in the pattern: People seemed to be separated according to their religion, and some religions were considered "better" than others.

By the time he had lived in Prescott for three years, Item Three in the pattern became clear to young Fiorello: there were two kinds of people in the world, the rich and the poor. In Prescott, the rich people were men like Mr. Powers, who owned the Model Gold Mine and a ranch on the Gila River; Bill Smith of the Smith Brothers Meat Market; and Bill Kelly, who used to be mayor.

There were also people so rich that they never came to Prescott, but everything they did or said was reported in the newspapers. Their names sounded powerful and important when you said them to yourself: Collis P. Huntington, Anson Phelps Stokes, E. H. Harriman. They owned thousands of acres of mining, railroad, and timber lands and huge sums of money that they could see and handle any time they wanted. They could hire thousands of people to work for them. Not even the rich people in Prescott were *that* rich.

There was also another kind of people in Prescott, those that owned nothing. Fiorello saw many of them when he walked along the construction route of the railroad coming down from Ashfork through Prescott on its way to Phoenix. They were mostly "foreigners," who dug, laid ties, bucked the backbreaking iron rails into line, lived in tents, and ate from tin plates. They came to Prescott in their rough-looking clothes to buy the things they couldn't find in the company commissary. Their money was welcome in the stores and saloons, but the townspeople looked on them with suspicion and spoke of them with contempt.

One day Achille brought home a hungry Italian railroad laborer whose right hand was wrapped in dirty bandages. Between gulps of Irene's fragrant home cooking, he told the La Guardias that he had lost two fingers in an accident on the job. The stranger explained that, under the law, the employer was not responsible for any injury his workers suffered. If a man wasn't able to work, he lost his job. If he needed medical care or faced starvation, that wasn't the employer's affair. Achille gave his unfortunate countryman a few dollars to help him to the next town and said to Fiorello, whose face showed concern, "Yes, my son, this is the kind of thing that happens to poor people."

This, then, was the reality of the headlines and editorials Fiorello read in the Sunday edition of the *New York World*, a big, important-looking newspaper he fetched for Papa every week from Ross's drugstore. It had a brightly colored comic sheet, "The Yellow Kid," which Fiorello read with great delight before he started homeward. But it was a stern, serious-minded newspaper. Its motto was "To afflict the comfortable and comfort the afflicted."

In the year of 1893, several million people, afflicted by unemployment, cold, hunger, and hopelessness, needed all the comforting they could get, which wasn't much. In Arizona, the copper and silver mines of Bisbee and Jerome, and the smelter at Clarkdale, were shut down. Railroad jobs were very scarce. The idle miners drifted into town, stayed a while, and then wandered eastward. The *New York World* said that people were suffering everywhere. The newspaper published shocking reports and indignant editorials. It printed angry cartoons in which thin, forlorn men stood at boarded-up factory doors on which there were signs saying "CLOSED."

Lying on the parlor floor one evening, with the *World* spread out before him, Fiorello cried out to the family, "Listen to this!" He read an anguished headline: THEY CRY FOR BREAD—SIGHT OF STEAMING LOAVES SETS FAMISHED WILD.

The report told how the newspaper had sponsored a big Broadway benefit show and had used the money it raised to distribute free bread to needy families. Mama looked up from her sewing with alarm in her eyes. "It comes and it goes and it comes again," she said.

"Yes," Achille muttered, "1873, 1884, 1893. Three panics in twenty years! They go and they come again."

"Why do we have panics?" Fiorello asked.

Achille seemed unsure of the reasons. "There are many explanations. Some say it is because the farmers do not have enough money to buy the goods that are made by the factories; so the factories close and the people in the cities do not have jobs. This means that the city workers have no money to buy what the farmers grow. If the farmers cannot pay their debts they have to give their farms to the bankers. Then they go to the cities to look for jobs in the factories, but the factories are closed."

"Are all these things true, Papa?"

"It is not easy to know. Rich men, like Mr. Jay Gould, say that this panic is the fault of the Government, because it interferes too much in the affairs of the important businessmen. They and their friends know what is best for the country, they say."

Fiorello looked questioningly at his father. Achille struggled and thrust out his arms in a gesture of helplessness:

"All I know is that when there is a panic Mr. Gould does not go hungry, but workers who have lost their jobs must stand in breadlines."

And that was part of the pattern, too.

The pattern went beyond Prescott. It covered the whole country. It worked out to the advantage of the rich and the disadvantage of the poor, in good times and in bad.

Whipple Barracks, however, did not feel the pinch. Everyone's Army pay came in regularly. Life followed a nice solid routine of drill, guard mount, and parade. Baton in hand, at the summer concerts ordered by the commanding officer, Papa looked very distinguished as he conducted the stirring compositions of Sousa, Gilmore, Verdi, and Offenbach. Fiorello was very proud of him.

In the late afternoons, from the edge of the parade ground, Fiorello could witness the ceremony of Retreat, which was always the same. The bugler, standing straight and proud, sounded the "Call to the Colors." A detail led by a corporal moved into position at the flagpole and the bugle sounded again. Nearby, the boom of the evening gun shattered the sunset calm. Then the bugler blew "Retreat" and Fiorello let his eyes follow the Stars and Stripes down the mast. The solemn ritual of respectful hands lowering the flag made him breathe deep and stand straight. It strengthened his feeling that he belonged to Whipple Barracks and the Eleventh Infantry Regiment.

For a few months, however, Fiorello's attention was turned toward another army, the unglamorous desperate legion of "General" Jacob S. Coxey of Massillon, Ohio. Coxey's Army was the challenge of the jobless and the dispossessed to the nation at large and to the Federal Government in particular. The number of unemployed had increased from 800,000 in the summer of 1893 to more than 3,000,000 in the spring of 1894, but little was done to relieve their plight. Coxey, a passionate adherent of the Populist movement, was a well-to-do businessman who could not endure his own prosperity while others went hungry. He proposed that the government should spend $500,000,000 for new roads in order to create thousands of jobs and to help to revive business. He called on the unemployed to march to Washington, D. C., to petition Congress for this relief measure. The unemployed responded. This army and its "radical" aims were a topic of daily conversation in Prescott. Some spoke of it with fear and scorn, others with sympathy, but no one could ignore it. At home, when he read about Coxey's progress in the *New York World*, the boy announced to his elders: "If I were a man I would go with him." He felt rewarded by his father's understanding nod. Fiorello was disturbed when he read in the Prescott *Journal Miner* that an armory in Springfield, Massachusetts, was shipping rifles to Washington "to protect the U. S. Treasury from any attack by the Coxeyites."

Studying Coxey's picture in the *New York World*, Fiorello was certain that this Populist crusader and his men had no bad intentions. The portrait showed a mild man with a small droopy mustache. His cutaway business suit and his neat bowler were signs of unmistakable respectability. Altogether, there was nothing in the picture to support the public image of Coxey which most newspapers were trying to create—that of a red-eyed Anarchist, a wild man and a rabble-rouser who was threatening to overthrow the Government.

Following months of preparation, the march began on Easter Day, 1894. Coxey, derisively dubbed "General" by the newspapers, started out from Massillon with a contingent of one hundred men who had rallied to his standard from upstate New York and elsewhere. Their commissary wagons and horses were supplied by Coxey from the livery stable he owned, at his own expense. To see him off on his momentous journey, Coxey's wife and small son rode with him in a light carriage as far as Canton, Ohio, the army's first resting place.

The marchers were plagued by rain, mud, snow, and cold, but in Pennsylvania they picked up more recruits. In Homestead, which had been the scene of deadly warfare between striking steel workers and an army of hired strikebreakers at Andrew Carnegie's steel plant less than two years before, the marchers were welcomed by some four thousand people plus a fife and drum corps.

Elsewhere, the Coxeyites were met by the local police or by hostile gangs of townspeople who tried to break up the march or force the marchers to take a detour around their community. Much of the time, however, they received food, shelter, friendship, and money from the ordinary people of the villages and cities through which they passed. Local officials and important community leaders also helped them on their way, more often out of fear than out of charity.

Other groups streamed and straggled across the continent

from San Francisco, Chicago, and other big cities, encountering
the same mixture of friendliness and hostility. They were thousands strong when they started, but they dwindled to hundreds
as they neared their goal. According to plan Coxey and his remaining followers arrived at the outskirts of Washington on May
1 to join forces with contingents from Iowa, Montana, and California. The combined groups, about six hundred men, entered
the city, led by Grand Marshal Carl Browne (a California poet),
a brass band, and a man carrying an American flag. Thousands of
spectators gathered to see this small group of jobless men who had
been described and denounced by the newspapers for months as
"foreign agitators and bomb-throwers."

Actually Coxey had taken great care not to give his critics
any excuse for such accusations. Browne named the army the
"Commonweal of Christ." Coxey permitted only native-born or
naturalized American citizens to join him.

Nevertheless, neither President Cleveland nor anyone of
major importance in Washington was willing to give them a
hearing. At the Capitol grounds they were confronted by a
solid rank of mounted policemen. The army paused and Coxey
took his stand to make a speech. He wanted to remind the
Government that the Constitution guaranteed the right of citizens to petition Congress for redress of grievances. Before he
could begin, he was arrested for the petty offense of walking on
the grass. And to make additionally clear the contempt of the
Government for Coxey, his followers, and their ideas, a District
of Columbia court sentenced him to twenty days in jail. The
army remained in Washington for a time, then straggled homeward, defeated but memorable.

When Fiorello read about Coxey's humiliating arrest, he
waved a pudgy fist and cried, "They should have let him speak!
If I were president, I would have let him speak!"

CHAPTER 3

The Rough Rider

No SELF-RESPECTING YOUTH ASPIRES TO BE THE EXACT
duplicate of anyone the world has known before, no matter how
great the model. The hero he worships is merely the man he
has chosen to measure himself against. The youth is confident he
will become his own particular kind of man and so make himself
not the imitator but the equal of the man he admires most. If
there was any man in Prescott whom Fiorello regarded as noble,
it was William Owen (Bucky) O'Neill.

He had a mind as well as a gun and adversaries respected his
abilities with both. He knew that the printing press was might-
ier than the six-shooter and he had a feeling, which grew with the
years, that Arizona should not be a territory for the quick en-
richment of shrewd, tough individuals, but a land carefully and
lovingly developed for the common good.

Between 1860, when he was born in St. Louis, and 1879,
when he drifted into the Territory from Washington, D. C.,
Bucky had learned to set type, take shorthand, and practice law.
At twenty, he could stand alongside the Phoenix city marshal and
outshoot and subdue a cavalcade of rampaging Texas cow-
hands. This was his idea of recreation. For a living, Bucky
worked on the *Phoenix Gazette*. He drifted south to a job on the
Epitaph in newly settled Tombstone, west to Hawaii, and back
to the Territory to become a court stenographer in Prescott in

1883. Two years later he started *Hoof and Horn*, a weekly in which ranchers published pictures of their stock brands and advertised their ownership of them to make life harder for cattle rustlers.

At twenty-six, Bucky won election to a local judgeship. He showed a genuine talent for municipal administration and was subsequently elected sheriff by a huge vote. Wearing his tin star he led a two-week manhunt across three hundred miles of wilderness to capture four cowboys who had held up an Atlantic & Pacific railroad train. Holding the office of tax assessor, however, he decided that the same railroad was getting away with civic murder. Murder was what the owners screamed when he presented them with a tax bill for almost one million dollars. Bucky considered this a very reasonable amount for the four-and-a-quarter million acres of land they had received from the Government free of charge.

The bill was never paid because Bucky was overruled by higher authorities. Thus, Bucky decided to become a higher authority himself—by running for the position of Territorial Delegate to Congress. Either the Democratic or the Republican Party would gladly have chosen him as their candidate, but he was fed up with their docile behavior toward the railroads, and their lack of concern for Arizona's ordinary people. He decided, instead, to become a Populist and to run on the ticket of the newly formed People's Party. He was defeated twice, in 1894 and 1896, but was later elected mayor of Prescott.

When the La Guardias came to town in 1892, Bucky O'Neill was already something of a living local legend. During Fiorello's six formative years in Prescott, it was inevitable that the boy should admire the man and be influenced by him, despite the difference of age and community standing that lay between them. It was the relationship between the sun and a growing tree.

Fiorello, one of his old teachers remembers, "always wanted to be a lawyer, and every lunch hour he would bolt his food and dash to the courthouse to listen to cases or even to be in that atmosphere." Inside, he heard legal arguments. Outside, on the courthouse steps, he heard debates on local and national politics. There was no lack of issues and, with twenty lawyers in town, most of whom aspired to political careers, there were many debaters, including the glamorous Bucky O'Neill. Fiorello watched mannerisms, remembered pithy turns of phrase and, above all, tried to weigh the value of the facts and ideas that came his way.

He heard that farmers of the Midwest and South, unemployed city workers of the East, and the Western cattle raisers and silver miners were looking to the radical program of the Populists to lead the country out of the continuing depression. Their national organization, the People's Party, formed in 1892, advocated a highway-building program to insure that "in times of great industrial depression, idle labor should be employed on public works." The Populists also called for Government ownership of the railroads, telegraph, and telephone systems, an income tax law, the eight-hour day for labor, and banking reforms which would reduce the influence of the rich in Government.

The biggest, most exciting issue was Free Silver. For every ten men who argued the matter on the courthouse steps, there was only one who really knew anything about economics and the complexities of money systems. But most of the people around Prescott knew from their own experience that it stood something like this:

The money system of the United States was based on gold, which was represented by paper bills and coins of less valuable metal. Farmers received only small amounts of money (representing gold) for large quantities of their produce. And since they had started their farms by borrowing money, they found it hard to keep up with their taxes and their mortgage payments. In fact, as the years went by, the farmers went deeper and deeper into debt.

This was a state of affairs, however, from which the banks and the big industrialists benefited. Since they owned or controlled most of the gold supply, they could pay low prices for the goods they bought and for the labor they hired. And they could charge high interest rates for the money they loaned to others. By 1893, so much of the actual money supply was in the hands of the big business interests that the economic life of the country came to a stop, the way a poker game peters out when one or two men have won all the chips.

Obviously, some new chips had to be put into the game. The Populists said that the way to do this was to have the Government buy as much silver as the nation's mines could produce and use it to mint more money. This would mean that a farmer would get a greater number of dollars for his crops and would have more money to pay his debts and buy the manufactured goods he needed. Money, in relation to goods, would be cheaper. In places like Prescott, where silver mining as well as farming and cattle raising were very important, this idea was particularly popular.

The issue of "cheap money" had been a lively one since the end of the Civil War, especially after the depression of 1893. People in Prescott had done their share of debating about Free Silver for several years. In the presidential contest of 1896, which Fiorello followed closely, William Jennings Bryan, the Populist-Democratic candidate, became the historic champion of Free Silver and ran against the Republican William McKinley, who supported Sound Money.

When November came, the Populists' choice, the great orator Bryan, lost the election. McKinley was sent to the White House and Fiorello was stunned. The score was close: seven million votes for the Republican and six-and-one-half million for Bryan, but the boy was not consoled.

Politics was to Fiorello as much of a hobby as stamp collecting was to other boys just turning fourteen. He may not have known everything there was to know about Free Silver but he memorized a good part of the resolution adopted at a convention in Phoenix to advocate statehood for Arizona. In the kitchen of their Whipple Barracks home, he declaimed it for his mother one morning while she stirred a pot of beans and macaroni:

"We have a population which is like the population of other states, intelligent, liberty-loving, and patriotic. It is a population practically free of lawlessness or a distinctively criminal element . . ."

Irene gazed affectionately at her son, studying his jet black hair, his dark eyes and healthy olive skin. "Ah, Fiorello," she said, "if you only knew your school work as well as you know what those politicians say . . ." Seeing the disappointment in his eyes, she retreated. "Go on," she smiled. "That's fine. Let's hear the rest." She was aware of the boy's strong appetite for ideas and for public expression of them.

Most children of that generation participated in school entertainment programs reluctantly, but Fiorello enjoyed his opportunities to be in the limelight. The years in Prescott provided him with a generous number of such big moments. At thirteen, he recited "The Adventure of a Cat" in a school program. In his fourteenth and fifteenth years he regaled audiences of parents and people who had nowhere else to go with renditions of the "Emily Polka," "The Last Rose of Summer," and selections from "Il Trovatore." As a family team, he and Gemma were occasionally mentioned in the *Journal Miner* and *Hoof and Horn* together with another celebrated local musician, Miss Queenie Potts.

Fiorello found his true forte, however, on the evening of January 28, 1898, when he completed his grammar school education with a class of six others. He was assigned to make a graduation speech and the subject he chose was prophetic: "The Office Seeker's Platform." Achille and Irene sat close to the stage. They listened with loving attention and were thrilled when Fiorello's teacher came forward to shake his hand. The rest of the audience was impressed. So was Fiorello.

The experience made him more certain that some time, not too far off, he would be able to measure up to men like Bucky O'Neill. He could think of nothing to prevent him from becoming a lawyer and maybe, in his time, running for mayor of Prescott. He and the O'Neills, Coxeys, and Bryans of this world saw eye to eye on the conflict between the affluent and the downtrodden. Furthermore, he was beginning to discover some new Items in the pattern that had revealed itself to him in his first years in Prescott. As matters stood, the pattern favored the rich and the powerful, but the important thing was that it could be changed. William Jennings Bryan and Bucky O'Neill wanted to be elected to office to rearrange the pattern. There were possibilities . . . but they were never to be realized in Prescott.

On the night of February 15, 1898, the United States battleship, *Maine*, exploded as she rode at anchor in Havana harbor.

Two hundred and sixty-six men and officers died. A U. S. Naval Court of Inquiry failed to fix responsibility, but it was generally assumed that the explosion was caused, either accidentally or on purpose, by a mine. Twenty-five years of increasingly bad relations with Spain, which held Cuba as a colony, had come to a head. National pride was outraged. Americans from coast to coast took up the cry "Remember the Maine." In land-locked Prescott there was talk about sending a big navy to drive Spain out of the Caribbean. War seemed inevitable and on April 26, Congress authorized President McKinley to make the fateful declaration.

The day after the *Maine* went down, Bucky O'Neill started recruiting a regiment of cowboys, miners, scouts, and others of Arizona's most rugged frontiersmen. So irrepressible was the eagerness of the volunteers that O'Neill's collaborator, Jim Mc-Clintock, had to send repeated appeals to Washington urging immediate induction of "Arizona's rough riding men." Two days after Congress voted for war, 210 of Bucky's one thousand volunteers were mustered in at Fort Whipple. That was all the Government would accept as Yavapai County's contribution to Arizona's elite regiment, the First U. S. Volunteer Cavalry which won fame as the "Rough Riders." The rest were turned away angry and chagrined. Mayor O'Neill became Captain O'Neill of Troop A by virtue of the commission which the Governor issued to him. On May 4, there was a public ceremony of farewell to the contingent. Judge Ling stepped forward and said to O'Neill, "You are now in the cavalry and the City of Prescott wishes to give you a mount. It's not full grown. It's merely a Colt . . ." Then he handed him a new revolver as the crowd cheered. Eight weeks later Bucky was killed by a Spanish sniper's bullet.

CHAPTER 4

From Tampa to Trieste

THE WAR PROCLAMATION THAT PUT THE ROUGH
Riders into uniform, signified action for the Eleventh Infantry
Regiment as well. The La Guardia family pulled up stakes
and said good-by to their comfortable Whipple Barracks parlor.
When Papa and the rest of the men went into training at Mobile,
Alabama, the women and children were moved to Jefferson Bar-
racks, St. Louis.

It was difficult for Fiorello to leave the only home town he
had ever known, particularly during his first high school term,
but he did not cry over spilled milk. St. Louis had attractions of
its own. One of these was a chance to seek enlistment in the
Army. Try as they would, sympathetic recruiting officers who
sized up the five-foot-one, baby-faced youth could not overlook
the fact that he was offering too little, too soon. They turned him
down.

For a few days, Fiorello consoled himself with his father's
parting admonition: "You are the man of the family now. From
Mobile the regiment will go to Tampa and then it will sail to
Cuba. You must take care of Mama and Gemma and Richard
until I come back."

It became increasingly clear to Fiorello, however, as the dull
inactive days dragged by, that Mama really didn't need much
help from him so long as the Army provided her with a home and

a Chief Musician's pay allotment for the family. The only thing around Jefferson Barracks that interested Fiorello was the telegraph office, which he haunted for news of the war in general and of Papa's regiment in particular. It was as though the clicking telegraph key was trying to say something to him. One day he understood the message. He hurried home and put on his best clothes. In reply to his mother's questioning looks, he explained, "I'm going into town to look for work. I'll be back in the afternoon."

"Watch out for the horsecars," she said. "St. Louis is a big city."

"Yes, Mama."

"And don't get too friendly with strangers. We are not in Prescott any more."

"I know, Mama."

Fiorello returned in the afternoon with startling news. "Mama," he said solemnly, "I'm going to war."

Irene was accustomed to earth-shaking announcements from her mercurial son.

"The Army didn't want you before," she smiled. "How did you make them change their minds?"

"Not the Army," said the boy, impatiently. "The *St. Louis Post-Dispatch*. I am a war correspondent, Mama."

"So-o-o. How much are they paying you?"

"So far, nothing," Fiorello explained. "I told the editor that all I wanted was my railroad fare to Mobile and credentials so I could get into camp with Papa."

Irene's expression grew somber. Her son was going.

"It wasn't easy," Fiorello exclaimed triumphantly. "I explained to the editor that I grew up in the Army and I could send him much better reports than some Eastern college dude who doesn't know a saddle horn from a bugle."

"You're gonna see Papa," Richard hollered. Gemma didn't say anything. Irene choked back her tears. She knew there was no point in trying to stop him. Her eager, teenage son had crossed his Rubicon. She could not ask him to turn back.

Even before he set out on his "assignment," St. Louis' youngest war correspondent saw some action, but he was the subject rather than the author of a story in the *Post-Dispatch*. There was a fire in Jefferson Barracks one night and the paper reported that "a bright boy and an exceptionally good cornetist ran into a blazing building for his cornet to blow the fire call." There was an accompanying picture of Fiorello with his cornet.

A few days later, the family went to the railroad station to say good-by to Fiorello, who was dressed for the occasion in an improvised correspondent's uniform of canvas leggings, civilian pants, a military looking tunic, and a genuine Army hat. He carried himself manfully and as he left, he admonished Richard and Gemma: "Take good care of Mama, do you hear? Do what she tells you."

From Mobile, he broke into print with a story headlined "The Post-Dispatch's Youthful Correspondent Heard From." His authorship was acknowledged but misspelled in a by-line which read "By F. LaGuardia." Of the troops in camp, the pint-size, under-age journalist wrote, "They are a nice lot of good spirited boys and the right sort of men to defend their country. They are ready and anxious for the orders to go to Cuba . . ." Many of them did go, but Fiorello and his father never got south of Tampa.

Achille left Mobile first. His son soon arrived and found the Florida embarkation port wallowing in an atmosphere of reckless gaiety that had nothing in common with the patriotic purpose he envisioned. No one who set foot in the city could fail to see its crowding, noise, rowdyism, and disorganization, both military and civilian. Bands in the street blared "There'll Be a Hot Time in the Old Town Tonight" and quartets from behind swinging saloon doors wailed the refrain.

By the time he found his way to the Quartermaster's hut in camp, Fiorello was eager for the reassuring sight of his father's face. "I'm looking for Chief Musician La Guardia, Eleventh Infantry," he said to the man on duty. "I'm his son."

The soldier looked at him, without answering. At last he said, "Well, young fella, your pa isn't feeling too good right now. I'll get somebody to take you to him."

Fiorello was totally unprepared for what he saw when he reached his father's bedside in the camp hospital. Papa's firm healthy flesh seemed to have melted away. He lay shrunken and wasted, his face waxen and hollow-cheeked. The eyes, staring at Fiorello with sad recognition, revealed a helplessness shockingly unlike the robust Papa he knew. His hand moved in a feeble gesture of greeting and Fiorello could contain himself no longer and burst into tears.

Achille had fallen victim to an enemy that took more American lives than the bullets of the Spanish sharpshooters in the Cuban hills. Like his comrades, he had eaten the tainted meat sold by unscrupulous meat packers and contractors to the U. S. Army. The meat was so full of unpleasant-tasting and probably injurious preservatives that the men called it "embalmed beef." This plus the bad camp sanitation and the lack of adequate measures to protect the troops from malaria and yellow fever killed almost four thousand soldiers. Fewer than four hundred were to die in battle. After the war ended, there were official investigations. A number of people were embarrassed but no one was officially dishonored or punished.

Slowly Achille struggled back to some semblance of health. The Army gave him his honorable discharge on August 22, 1898, for "disease of the stomach and bowels, catarrh of head and throat, and malarial poisoning." Father and son made a cheerless, tiring journey to rejoin the rest of the family at Jefferson Barracks. En route, they talked. Achille was bitter. Fiorello was depressed and angered by what he had seen. Saving the Cuban people from Spanish oppression was one thing; they weren't sorry about that. Profiteering at the expense of the men in the ranks was another matter. It was criminal. But the voice and gestures in which Achille condemned the Beef Trust and the War Department bunglers, lacked the old vigor. Fiorello listened and watched his father's face. He felt a new responsibility.

The family examined the possibility that it might be a long time before Achille could find civilian work. Worse, now that they were no longer an Army family, they would be homeless. Their cash resources amounted to a few hundred dollars in savings and a monthly eight-dollar disability pension from the War Department. Achille saw only disaster ahead unless they all moved to Trieste and remained near Mama's people until he

could get on his feet again. Fiorello agreed but he promised himself he would return as soon as he could. Whatever ties he might
have overseas, he had grown up as an American and America was
where he meant to live.

CHAPTER 5

Our Man in Fiume

ACHILLE LA GUARDIA'S EIGHTEEN YEARS OF MUSICAL adventuring in America had ended on something less than a note of triumph, but he was not ready to accept defeat. At fifty, he turned resolutely to the task of building a new life for himself and his family in Trieste.

For a while the family lived with Grandma Coen, the Fiorina after whom Fiorello was named. Achille's first enterprise, a carting business, was short-lived. It called for more stamina than his continuing ill health allowed. With Fiorello's help, he then tried his hand as a provisioner of passenger ships docking in Trieste, which was Austria's port on the Adriatic.

After this period of trial and error, Achille hit his stride, in 1900, by leasing a small hotel at the seaside resort of nearby Capodistria. Mama did the bookkeeping; Gemma, wearing a large, impressive ring of keys, supervised the bed-making and the wine cellar, and Richard did the heavy work. Papa ran the kitchen, conducted a five-piece ensemble that provided dinner music for the guests, and at suitable moments he played the gracious host, going from table to table and making interesting conversation in a variety of languages.

Just when things were faring so well that he was preparing to buy the place outright, Achille died, on October 21, 1904. He had never fully recovered from his illness in Tampa. The hotel was abandoned. Richard went off to become a ship's interpreter. Irene and Gemma went to Fiume to live with Fiorello. But why had Fiorello gone to Fiume?

During the first two years after the family's arrival from the United States, Fiorello had helped Papa as much as he could and had spent his free time learning how to live in his European environment. He picked up new languages, German, French, and Croatian, the way scouts and prospectors picked up Indian dialects in Arizona—by ear and by eagerness. His Italian flourished and he even acquired some Yiddish. In 1900, the year that the family moved to the Capodistria hotel, Fiorello went to Budapest to be a clerk in the U. S. Consulate. He landed the job with the help of his father's friend, Raymond Willey, a consular agent.

At eighteen, Fiorello was out on his own. He was ambitious, energetic, and smart. His obscure job in the service of Uncle Sam seemed as good a way as any for a young man to cross the threshold of a new century.

From the bottom of the ranks of clerks in the Budapest office, he rose rapidly despite his youth and lack of education. After a scant three years, he was put in charge of the consular agency in Fiume, which is to say, in charge of himself. It was a one-man office. In February, 1904, two months after his twenty-first birthday, he received an official commission as a U. S. consular agent. The salary was $800 a year plus free rent for a suite of two rooms which served as office and bedroom.

Fiume, some forty miles overland from Trieste, was Hungary's only seaport. From its docks as many as two thousand emigrants sailed for New York every two weeks on the Cunard and Adria Lines. During his time there, Fiorello was responsible for overseeing the passage of some ninety thousand emigrants from the Old to the New World.

To everyone concerned, the United States and European governments, and the steamship lines, it was perfectly satisfactory that a young man of twenty-one have so much authority over the movement of the ships and passengers that made up the huge emigration traffic. No one expected him to use his authority, but Fiorello had developed some ideas of his own during his

consular apprenticeship. It struck him that there was too much
concern about clearance papers, manifests, and sailing schedules,
and too little interest in the steady stream of hopeful people who
had cut themselves off from their homelands to take their chances
in America.

The health regulations Fiorello was supposed to enforce
were intended less for the benefit of the emigrants than for the
protection of the steamship lines from financial loss. Obviously
sick persons were not allowed to sail, but others, with less easily
detectable diseases, such as trachoma, were turned away from
New York after their long voyage by U. S. Immigration Service
doctors, as the Federal law required. His remedy for this tragic
situation was worthy of Bucky O'Neill. One morning, he turned
up aboard a Cunard liner with a doctor and ordered the ship's
captain to line up the emigrants for medical inspection. The Cunard Line agent made horrified protests. Consular officers *never*
supervised medical examinations in person, he insisted.

"This one does," said La Guardia.

"I have no instructions from my superiors to permit this pro-
cedure," the agent argued.

"You don't need any instructions. No inspection, no clearance papers," the consular spokesman snapped. So saying, he left
the ship, with the doctor at his heels.

The distress signals sent up by the Cunard Line were seen
in London and Washington, but the U. S. State Department
made a ruling that supported La Guardia's position. Thereafter,
every emigrant from the port of Fiume who had a disease that
could bar him from entry to the United States was saved the disappointment and the ruinous cost of a boat ride to nowhere. And
when the young consular officer informed the steamship lines
that they would have to pay the doctor's fees for the inspections,
they didn't argue very long. They paid.

Even in those days, Fiorello cared more about beneficial
results for human beings than he did for protocol. No sooner
did he arrive in Fiume than he prevented a Croatian-born American citizen from being drafted into the Hungarian army. He
was reprimanded by his superior, Frank Dyer Chester, the con-

sular chief in Budapest, for the rambunctious way he went about it. Fiorello replied that if he had waited, the victim would have been in uniform and beyond diplomatic help.

In the spring of 1904, Fiorello La Guardia—age 21; height, 5 feet, 2 inches; weight, 124 pounds; and political influence, o— engaged in another test of strength with the Austro-Hungarian Empire.

The occasion was the visit of her Imperial Highness, the Archduchess Maria Josefa of Austria, to the port of Fiume. The city was tidied up to look its Sunday-best and its officials spared neither pains nor imagination to provide entertainment for the exalted lady of the House of Hapsburg. Since there were about five hundred emigrants waiting to sail to the United States on the steamship *Panonia*, it was decided that her Highness might be amused by the spectacle of these low-born creatures trudging up the gangplank wearing their holiday dress and dragging their luggage.

The ship's captain, the Governor General, and the other authorities made all the necessary arrangements, which did not include, of course, any consultation with the emigrants themselves. The only missing detail was the bill of health without which ships carrying emigrants could not enter an American port; and the only man who could issue the document was consular agent La Guardia.

Fiorello refused on the grounds that the ship was not scheduled to sail for three days. The law, he pointed out, required that steerage passengers be put aboard ships as close to sailing time as possible. It would be brutal as well as illegal to herd the passengers into their crowded quarters below decks and let them swelter there for three days and three nights.

La Guardia's flat refusal triggered a campaign of pressure to make him change his mind. A blizzard of soft words and hard threats swirled around him. He was even invited to tea by the Archduchess on board the *Panonia* to watch the parade of peasants from the ship's bridge. He refused without apologies. When somebody said that the Austro-Hungarian government would make things difficult for him in Washington, he jutted out his lower lip and said, "Tell the Archduchess she can boss her own people but she can't boss the American consul."

At that point, he decided that the best way to handle the situation was to disappear. The officer of the port of Fiume and a task force of assorted functionaries hunted for him all day and were unsuccessful. There was one place they didn't dream of looking. Fiorello was in the home of the port officer, having tea with the official's charming wife and listening to her play the piano. Maria Josefa never did see the embarkation of the *Panonia*'s steerage passengers. It was wonderful what a man wielding authority could do when he was fighting on the side of the angels.

If Fiorello managed to horrify a mighty monarchy by his official behavior, he also succeeded in winning a certain amount of respect for his Arizona-style defense of Austro-Hungarian womanhood one winter in Fiume. During the carnival season he went to a masked ball with some of his dashing young friends among the military and the civilians. It was the custom at these romantic events for ladies to dance, dine, and permit themselves to be escorted to their carriages or to their very doors by gentlemen they might never have met before, without unmasking. The idea was that since the mask made the lady anonymous, her flirtations at the ball could not be deemed socially improper.

On leaving the ball, Fiorello and a young lady with whom he had danced and flirted all evening, were stopped by her angry fiancé who tried to tear the mask from her face. The young loser of numerous bareknuckle bouts in the Prescott schoolyard knocked the interloper down. The man picked himself up, handed Fiorello his card, and said, "My seconds will call on you in the morning." Fiorello prepared himself for the encounter, but Fiorello's and the fiancé's seconds got together and drew up a document which satisfied everyone's sense of honor, and made the duel unnecessary. The incident had a doubly happy ending because the young lady later married one of Fiorello's seconds.

Less than a year after he took over in Fiume, Fiorello wrote to Washington expressing his opinion that his office should be changed from a branch of the Budapest headquarters to a full consulate in its own right and that he ought to be promoted to the rank of full consul. Washington didn't promote him because of the reports Frank Dyer Chester had been obliged to make. Although, he wrote of Fiorello as the most able man on his staff, he sometimes found it necessary to complain to Washington of the young consular agent.

Fiorello thought nothing, for example, of going over Mr. Chester's head by writing directly to bureaus of the U. S. Treasury and Commerce Departments. He had also succeeded in insulting Count Szapari, the Governor General of Fiume, and he did not mince words with lesser dignitaries.

Nevertheless, America's most undiplomatic diplomat in Europe continued to do his job with great ability and to wait for advancement with growing impatience. By 1906, it became clear that his chances of getting ahead didn't amount to much. He discussed the matter with Mr. Chester. The well-born, well-to-do man from Harvard broke it as gently as possible to Fiorello that without the advantages of a Harvard education, Mayflower ancestors, and money of his own, there was no future for him in the service of the State Department.

Fiorello decided it was time for a showdown. He asked to be made Consul General at Belgrade. "If knowledge of the language and six years of service are not sufficient to counterbalance his total lack of political influence," Fiorello wrote, "the undersigned begs for a special examination or appointment to a post within the United States. If none of the above can be practically granted, there remains no doubt that this is not the place for a young man to work up." The State Department was unmoved and Fiorello resigned on May 31, 1906.

Irene was dismayed when she heard of Fiorello's resignation. It was a lovely job, with a good salary and some importance. After all, how many people in Fiume were paid for challenging steamship agents and officials of the Austro-Hungarian Empire?

"Mama," he told her, "my work is getting too easy and too monotonous. If I stay here, I won't be any better off when I'm sixty-five than I am now. I'm going back to America, where I belong."

Mama went to live with Gemma, who had married Herman Gluck, a Jewish bank clerk, in Budapest. Fiorello took a job as a steward on the *S.S. Ultonia* and sailed for New York after bluntly refusing Mr. Chester's request to stay until June 30, the end of the bookkeeping year.

When Fiorello returned to America, he was twenty-three years old. He knew his strength and lost no sleep over his weaknesses. He returned to America because he wanted to complete his education, become a lawyer, and in his own words, "enter public service." But what did "public service" mean? To La Guardia it meant having governmental authority and using it for the benefit of those who needed help, no matter how the people in power complained. Poor people did not seem able to do very much for themselves, either in Prescott or in Fiume, La Guardia had observed. What they needed was a man who couldn't endure injustice to others, a man who was not afraid to take the "do not disturb" sign off the door of solid privilege. Fiorello knew that he was such a man, and he hungered for the power which would enable him to prove it.

CHAPTER 6

A University Called New York

FOR A YOUNG MAN OF LA GUARDIA'S ABILITIES, AMBI-
tions, and antecedents, there was no better place than New York
in 1906, a fact of which he became convinced after spending a
month in Portsmouth, Ohio.

Raymond Willey, who had helped him once before, found
a job for him there in a brick factory, but the Ohio River town
offered no opportunities for the kind of schooling Fiorello
wanted.

Returning to his native Greenwich Village in New York, he
found temporary employment at $10 a week with the Society
for the Prevention of Cruelty to Children as a translator of
French documents, then moved on to $15 a week as a clerk for a
steamship company. Meanwhile, he invested $7.50 in a six weeks'
shorthand course at Pratt Institute. When he finished, he was
hired by Abercrombie & Fitch as a stenographer at $20 a week.

Now his race to catch up on his education began in earnest.
He attended a "cram" school at night which would help him pass
the New York State Regents Examinations and qualify him for a
Federal civil service appointment. Time flew. Fiorello hardly noticed when 1906 became 1907 or when the new winter turned
into another summer. He could spare no time for the social life
he had pursued so pleasantly in Fiume. Perhaps his only social

life was his regular visits to Frank Giordano's one-chair barber-shop at Sixth and Greenwich Avenues.

The two men were close friends. Frank, a year younger than his favorite customer, was almost six feet tall, broad-shouldered, deep-chested. His resonant baritone was soothing when he spoke and delightful when he sang Neapolitan songs, usually while working up the lather in a shaving mug. Although in the U. S. for five years, his biggest step toward Americanization was to acquire the name of Frank. His customers called him Chich, the colloquial Italian form of Francisco.

Fiorello looked forward to his almost daily ritual of being shaved, hearing Giordano's songs, and conversing with him in Italian, a language which he had not known well when he had sailed for Europe. Despite eight years abroad, he remained intensely, proudly American, but he had begun to carry his Italian heritage freely and candidly. He had little choice. Americans of Anglo-Saxon stock saw more of the Adriatic than of Arizona in his short, slim figure, his straight black hair, and his oval face with the dark, deep-set eyes. Immigrants claimed him as one of their own because he spoke their language, lived among them, and reacted to them with none of the restraint they sensed in the behavior of most native Americans. Chich was flattered by the friendliness of this Italianized American who earned his living in a dignified white-collar occupation. Fiorello was soothed and gratified by the mixture of comradeship and respect with which the young barber treated him. One was a natural leader, the other an admiring follower.

Early one September evening in 1907, Fiorello burst into Giordano's shop. His step was brisk and his straw hat was cocked jauntily. The place was empty. Fiorello bounded into the high leather-covered chair and yelled, "Hey, Chich! How about a haircut?"

Giordano came out from behind the limp calico curtain that screened off his living quarters at the back of the shop. While Chich arranged his tools, Fiorello studied his features in the mirror.

"Stop looking," Giordano said in Italian. "You need a shave, too."

Fiorello looked at him sharply. "Chich," he said, "you're no good."

"What's eating you?" Giordano asked.

"You've been in this country five years, Chich, and I'll bet you don't know more than ten words of English."

"What of it? All my customers speak Italian."

"That's only an excuse for being lazy. How do you expect to make something of yourself without knowing English?"

"Don't worry about me. . . . Sit up straight."

"Chich, I'm going to stop talking Italian to you. Then you will have to begin learning."

"You're joking."

Both of them knew it was an empty threat. The language was a cherished bond between them.

To change the subject, Fiorello asked, "How's business?"

"Not good," Giordano replied. "When people don't have jobs they don't spend money in the barbershop. Everyone says it is a panic."

"Things will get better, Chich. Since we were born, it's happened at least three times before."

"But meanwhile people have no money for rent. They can't pay the grocery bill."

"I know."

"What are we to do?"

"Elect strong honest men to office," shouted Fiorello. "Send real representatives of the people to Washington, Albany, City Hall. Men like Teddy Roosevelt, dammit."

"But Teddy Roosevelt *is* in Washington. He is the President."

"That's all right. We need more like him."

"And maybe men like Fiorello La Guardia?"

"Sure, why not? You think only an Irishman can get anywhere in politics? You'll see!"

"Good, good!" said Giordano. "I will vote for you. Many people will vote for you. You will get elected."

"Aha!" Fiorello laughed. "How will you be able to vote for anybody if you don't know the English language?"

"Never mind, I will learn," Giordano muttered.

There was silence for a few minutes. Then Fiorello said: "Listen, Chich. I want to tell you something. You know why I'm getting my hair cut now?"

"No. Why?"

"I'm going over to New York University to register at the Law School. I'm going to study at night. In two or three years, I will be a lawyer, an *avvocato*."

Giordano growled his approval and pumped his customer's hand. "Fiorello," he said, "*buona fortuna*."

The good fortune that followed Fiorello for the next three years consisted largely of work and study, with an occasional evening out among the friends he was able to make despite his lack of leisure. In November, 1907, he became an interpreter on Ellis Island at one hundred dollars a month, a respectable salary in those days. Because immigrants were arriving at the rate of some 55,000 a month, Fiorello was on duty seven days a week. He began work at nine o'clock in the morning, caught a five-thirty ferryboat in the evening, ate a hasty dinner, did what homework he could, and went to his classes.

He was not too busy, however, to feel pain and anger at the daily spectacle of the hardships imposed on the new arrivals by the inconsistencies and omissions of the immigration laws. There was a law which excluded immigrants with contracts to work. This was intended to protect them against unscrupulous exploitation by labor contractors and employers. There was another law which excluded immigrants without prospects of a job, to keep them from becoming public charges. Fiorello wrote letters to Congress, complaining about this contradiction.

Families were still being separated or sent back to their homelands destitute, because one member, often a child, had trachoma, or some other disqualifying disease. Fiorello wrote letters to Congress urging a law requiring the thorough physical examination of immigrants at the port from which they were sailing, as he had done in Fiume. It was not until 1919 that his proposal did become a law.

His duties took him to City Hall to help immigrant couples get married. The fees for the marriage license and the civil ceremony, usually exorbitant, were an established part of the graft garnered by Tammany aldermen legally empowered to perform the civil ceremony. Fiorello was indignant at the insulting manner in which the officials, often only half sober, conducted what should have been a solemn ritual.

At Night Court, which he had attended as interpreter for immigrants in trouble with the law, he saw judges, policemen, lawyers, bail bondsmen, all eager to make every dollar they could from the misfortunes of these recent arrivals. Before his first visit to Night Court, one of his superiors, Andrew Tedesco, told him: "You can get experience in this job or you can make a great deal of money. I don't think you'll take the money. But remember, the test is if you hesitate. Unless you say No! right off, the first time an offer comes your way, you're gone."

Fiorello was not the hesitating type. He hesitated neither in his conviction that those who prospered on the exploitation of immigrants and the native poor had no place in public life, nor in his resolution that when he got the chance he would make things hot for such "tinhorns."

He didn't think twice, either, about asking for a raise because of his language abilities, his stenographic training, and consular service background. By the time his request was granted, however, he was getting ready for his final exams at law school. He received his degree as Bachelor of Laws in June, 1910, and was admitted to the bar that fall. He was twenty-eight years old, unmarried, and ready to make the world come to terms with him.

CHAPTER 7

The Lawyer and the Tiger

WITH SIXTY-FIVE DOLLARS TO HIS NAME, LA GUARDIA resigned from the Immigration Service. Then he rented office space from McIlheny & Bennett, an established firm with a good law library, and had a sign painted on the door of his small room:

FIORELLO H. LA GUARDIA
Counsellor-at-Law

He wrote to his mother on his new stationery, explaining that the middle initial stood for Henry, the English form of Enrico, his hitherto little-used middle name.

For Fiorello, as a young lawyer, the times were lean. The rejection of small opportunities to fatten his pocketbook caused his colleagues to shake their heads at his foolhardiness.

One of the cases he rejected concerned an old Italian lady whose son had been arrested on a criminal charge. Fiorello listened carefully to her tearful account then told her very gently, as was his way with old people and children: "Mama, your boy gets into trouble so often that I think it would do him good to spend some time in jail. I would like to help you but, I'm sorry, I can't take your case."

A butcher came to him demanding that his neighbor, a greengrocer, be brought to court for cluttering up the sidewalk

with vegetable crates. La Guardia heard the aggrieved shop-
keeper's long, loud recital and astounded him by saying, "If you
were less stubborn you could settle your quarrel without a lawyer. It's much cheaper and easier that way."

The butcher went to another lawyer, but he complained to
his friends about La Guardia's rebuff. The stories of the cases La
Guardia refused to take began to circulate and with them went
word that there was an honest young lawyer down at 15 William
Street who wasn't out to put the squeeze on poor people in need
of help.

During that early period of his practice, he undertook to defend the victim of a police "frame up," a man falsely accused of
robbery. La Guardia worked without pay because he was sure of
the man's innocence. The more he studied the case the more
enraged he became. He began to feel that an innocent man who
had money could stay out of jail more easily by bribing the arresting officer, the prosecuting attorney, and the judge—all Tammany appointees—than he could by hiring a lawyer.

In court, Fiorello pleaded convincingly, but nobody wanted
to be convinced. Judge, prosecutor, and witnesses went through
the motions of convicting his client with the mechanical preci-
sion of a professional football team scoring against a bunch of
neighborhood scrubs. The young attorney left the courtroom
furious.

People still talked of *The Shame of the Cities*, a book in
which Lincoln Steffens, a journalist with a passion for civic decency, had collected the facts about crooked government in the
big American cities. The book merely supplied chapter and verse
for the common understanding that political machines had become what historian Charles A. Beard later called "a special form
of business enterprise" from which politicians made huge sums
of money by their administration of the city governments.

Fiorello had no illusions about how these machines operated.
In some cities they were Republican, in others Democratic, and
in still others, control of the city administration shifted back and
forth. In most of the cities, the two groups co-operated with each
other.

The ruling New York machine was Tammany, which had

started out before 1800 as a social, charitable, and patriotic society. After the Civil War, the Tammany appetite for tribute became so great and its power so fearsome that the cartoonist
Thomas Nast began to portray the organization as a tiger. The
symbol endured. By the beginning of the twentieth century,
Tammany had become the biggest "business enterprise" of its
kind. Its large building on Fourteenth Street was a sort of black
market where everything connected with municipal government
had a price, from a police sergeant's stripes to a multimillion-dol-
lar contract for building a bridge. Tammany Hall was the real
headquarters of New York's political and governmental power.
The graceful City Hall farther downtown was the annex.

It was natural for Attorney La Guardia, barely out of law
school in 1910, to join the Republican Club of the Twenty-Fifth
Assembly District in which he lived. His motive had little to do
with eagerness to build up his practice. He was itching for a
chance to challenge Tammany Boss Charlie Murphy's "special
form of business enterprise."

When he told Chich Giordano that he had taken the plunge,
the barber said, "Good. They are not so crooked as Tammany,
hey?"

Fiorello frowned. "A machine is a machine, Republican or
Democrat. In this district we're kind of lucky. We've got a smart
bunch of high class goo-goos running the organization."

"Goo-goo" was the sneering name given by entrenched politicians to those who entered politics for the sake of good government. It was a period when many middle- and upper-class Americans had become so sickened by political corruption that they
decided to make themselves personally responsible for cleaning
up the nation's civic life. A few of them joined the Socialist
Party. One of them, New York State Senator Franklin D. Roosevelt, had come into minor prominence as the leader of a small
group of Democrats bucking Tammany domination within their
party. Most of them, however, were following the pattern of
"clean politics" as practiced by Theodore Roosevelt, Franklin's
older cousin. T.R. became a politician and a vigorous president.
He believed that as a wealthy scion of the nation's oldest aristoc-
racy, the New York Dutch, he had a moral obligation to take a

direct hand in government. He considered success in politics as much of a challenge to his manhood as roughing it in the Dakotas. To leave the job of government to his uncouth "inferiors" the full-time ward heelers, would have been lazy and cowardly.

For his time, and in comparison with his presidential predecessors, McKinley, Cleveland, and Harrison, Teddy Roosevelt was a liberal. He advocated many reforms and succeeded in making some of them the law of the land. During earlier administrations, the railroads and the trusts had rolled ruthlessly over the American economy, enriching themselves fabulously at the expense of the farmer, the city worker, the small businessman, and the public treasury. Condemned by some and applauded by others as a ferocious radical, T.R.'s aim was merely to bring Big Business, grown avaricious, back to its senses. The speeches he made and the legislative steps he took to accomplish this won almost universal enthusiasm and respect during his seven years in the White House. He was hailed as the "Trust Buster" and the champion of the "Square Deal" for the common man. Politically, he was what prizefight circles call a crowd pleaser.

Teddy Roosevelt's philosophy and ripsnorting style had a natural appeal to Fiorello. They reminded him of the days of Bucky O'Neill and encouraged him to hope for the day when he could strike mighty blows for good government in his own right.

Nevertheless, when the Republican Party renominated President Taft in 1912 and T.R. decided to run against him on the "Bull Moose" ticket of the newly formed Progressive Party, Fiorello did not join the Roosevelt forces. Instead, he took over the captaincy of an election district vacated by an insurgent who left the club to campaign for the "Trust Buster."

The goo-goo dominated Republican Club of the Twenty-Fifth A.D. was strongly organized. It included wealthy men who knew how to turn their Ivy League college education and their privileged social position to practical advantage in the no-holds-barred battles of New York politics. There were Yale men Herbert Parsons and Henry H. Curran; Francis Stoddard, Harvard '98; Ezra P. Prentice, a Princeton alumnus; and Frederick C. Tanner, a Mayflower descendant and a son of a college president. They knew how to get down in the mud with the opposition and come up only slightly smudged.

Because they understood the difference between the Union League Club and the Twenty-Fifth A.D., these newcomers worked shoulder to shoulder with plebeians such as old Mike Kehoe, a shrewd political campaigner and Civil War veteran who was reputed to be drawing pensions from both the Federal Government and a Southern state; Harry Andrews, son of a poor English-German family; and Louis Espresso, an American of Italian immigrant parentage.

Fiorello learned the techniques of sidewalk politics from all three, but he identified himself most readily with Louis because of their similarities in ancestry, background, and age. The short, sturdily-built Espresso with the cold, sharp eyes and bulldog chin was different from his ward heeling opposites in Tammany in one respect. He was tired of seeing the Italian immigrants and their children in the role of permanent underdog.

Espresso was a "fixer" who knew how to help people out of trouble with the law. He helped the poor with baskets of groceries. He could obtain a pushcart license and sometimes a job for the head of a needy family. By such favors, he controlled a block of votes which he turned over to his party leaders on Election Day. For this service, the Republican bosses guaranteed the prosperity of his bail bond business and the small saloon he eventually bought. He did not aspire to public office. He was content to be a ward heeler keeping his eyes open all year "for the good of the party."

It was to Espresso that La Guardia first confided his intention of running for Congress. "That's not a very smart idea," said Louis. Another club leader had said to Espresso only a short time before, "Keep away from that La Guardia guy. He's a wild one." Louis ignored the suggestion because he could see a valuable ally in Fiorello. Anyway, he liked him.

"Fiorello," said Espresso, "forget it. An Italian will never get elected around here. You can make more money by sticking to your law practice and working for the party in your own neighborhood. And now that you know the ropes you can always pick up something extra."

La Guardia kept his thoughts to himself. Louis would never understand that he was not interested in making money. Fiorello didn't tell him that for years he had been a secret and studious reader of the *Congressional Record*. He merely said, "I just got a retainer from the garment workers union."

"You mean they've got money?" Louis smiled. The union in this winter of 1912-13 was involved in a desperate strike. Handling its unpopular cause in the courts was not likely to make a young lawyer rich.

"Louis," Fiorello replied, digging his forefinger into his colleague's chest, "some smart politician *you* are. Maybe they haven't got much money but they've got plenty of votes. They're going to *win* this strike and I'm going to help them. Louis, get it through your head that trade unions are here to stay. Do you know how many Italians and Jews become United States citizens every year? Hah!"

Representing labor unions was the kind of law practice Fiorello loved. It put him directly into the fight for the underdog and broadened his reputation as a man of political capabilities. The employers were trying to set the two major nationality groups in the needle trades, Jews and Italians, against each other. Undercover agents of the employers told each group that the other was ready to desert the union and go back to work. "The Jews are going back to work," they told the Italians; "The Italians are selling you out," they said to the Jews.

La Guardia made dozens of rousing speeches in Yiddish and Italian to convince each group that the other was loyal and that they could win the strike by sticking together. His words fell on willing ears. These workers had found it intolerable to work ten and twelve hours a day, twenty weeks a year, at top speed for low wages, and to live the rest of the time in jobless anxiety.

The lawyer spent his days in court defending arrested pickets and worked late into the night with union leaders planning strategy and fighting the antagonism displayed by the courts.

One magistrate even said: "You are on strike against God and nature, whose law is that man shall earn his bread by the sweat of his brow. You are on strike against God!"

He exhorted the strikers to defy all attempts to stop their

peaceful picketing. The little man in the dark suit, with a shock
of hair falling over his forehead, shot his fist skyward and
shouted, "I will be on the picket line with you tomorrow! Hard
work is a good thing, but long hours and low wages in a disease-
infested sweatshop leaves no time for a decent life." His angry
voice strained till it broke into a high scream, "God never intended a man to live like a dumb animal!"

He was as good as his word. The brisk little figure (lean
then, and not rotund and bandy-legged as newspaper photo-
graphs showed him twenty-five years later) appeared on the
picket line in front of an important garment factory the next
morning. He defied the police to arrest him. He begged them to
arrest him. He explained to them in a shrill, taunting voice that
he wanted them to come to court with him to see if they really
had the right to interfere with peaceful picketing. Nothing happened. They knew who he was and Tammany's policemen were
superstitious about arresting lawyers.

The strike was won. When the garment workers went back
to their jobs the work week was fifty-three hours instead of sixty;
factory sanitation was somewhat improved and they had won a
wage increase. La Guardia was one of three men chosen by the
union to work out the terms of the agreement with the employers. The strike gave Fiorello more than clients. It gave him followers.

CHAPTER 8

Congressman, I Love You

THE TRAMP OF GERMAN JACKBOOTS ON BELGIAN earth in August, 1914, produced little apprehension on the western side of the Atlantic. Americans took note of the conflict with the comfortable curiosity of bystanders.

In the Fourteenth Congressional District, largely populated by Europeans and their immediate descendants, there was less apathy because of personal loyalties or antagonisms toward the contending powers. But even among these immigrant groups the prospect of American involvement was unthinkable. Fiorello La Guardia knew better. He had encountered at first hand the clashing ambitions of the major European governments and the deep hatreds nursed by the minor nationalities during his Adriatic years.

Meanwhile, La Guardia was preoccupied with the affairs of the Twenty-Fifth A.D. Republican Club. This evening the headquarters hall was filled with men and tobacco smoke. The "boys" in the back room were lining up their slate for the September primary, which would designate the party's candidates in the November election. From his table where the nominating petitions were spread, acting leader Clarence Fay asked, "Who wants to run for Congress?"

"I do," said La Guardia, keeping his voice well below an eager shout.

"Okay," said Fay, "put La Guardia down." It was as simple as that. The man who was writing in the candidates' names called out, "Hey La Guardia, what's your first name?"

"Fiorello," said the would-be candidate.

The man poised his pen above the paper then looked up. "Ah, let's get someone whose name we can spell."

It was a moment which might have slipped from the grasp of a lesser man but La Guardia replied, with excellent timing and professional calm, "Just a minute, I'll spell it for you: F-I-O-R-E-L-L-O." There followed a brisk argument between the man with the pen and the man with the dream. Finally, the name of Fiorello H. La Guardia was inscribed on the petition as Republican candidate for the House of Representatives from the Fourteenth Congressional District, which sprawled clear across Manhattan from the East to the Hudson Rivers and from Fourth Street north to Fourteenth Street.

What gave Fiorello the edge in his dispute with the clubhouse clerk was the fact that in his four years of activity in the Twenty-Fifth A.D. he had won the respect of such local "influentials" as Mike Kehoe, Louis Espresso, and Harry Andrews, to say nothing of State Chairman Tanner and New York County Chairman Sam Koenig. In any case, no one else wanted the dubious honor of being a setup for the Tammany candidate, Michael Farley, saloon-keeper and president of the National Liquor Dealers Association, who was sure to win.

There was an unwritten "live and let live" arrangement between the opposing political machines. The Republicans, powerful in most of New York State, refrained from offering any real challenge to Tammany on its home grounds in New York City and vice versa. This saved a lot of time and unpleasantness. It also permitted each machine to cultivate its own "special form of business enterprise" with a minimum of inconvenience and a maximum of profit.

Fiorello was almost the only Republican in Manhattan who took his candidacy seriously. He arrived at his first election rally with political facts and oratorical fire, but he was not called on to speak. When he protested to his "coach," Mike Kehoe, the old campaigner bluntly told him, "You haven't got a chance, Fiorello. It's in the bag for Mike Farley. You get out there and campaign for the other boys, and one of these days you'll get nominated for something you can win."

Espresso and Andrews were of the same opinion, but when they saw that Fiorello insisted on running for election, they became his campaign managers. Kehoe said, "Okay, what's there to lose. Go ahead and try."

For about a hundred dollars, the candidate bought a beat up Ford and plastered it with the biggest signs it could carry:

VOTE FOR FIORELLO H. LA GUARDIA
FOR CONGRESS

He toured his predominantly immigrant and working-class district telling voters in Italian and Yiddish, as well as English, about his work on behalf of immigrants in Europe and Ellis Island; about his fight for the rights of labor in the garment workers' strike; about his devotion to good government. He wore out his shoes climbing stairways and calloused his knuckles knocking on doors to solicit the votes of the tenement dwellers. He attended weddings, christenings, funerals, fraternal society picnics, and clambakes to outhandshake the Tammany masters of the handshaking technique.

Tammany, accustomed to playing rough, received a dose of its own medicine from this upstart politician. He deluged the district with circulars bearing a flattering picture of himself and the worst one he could find of Michael Farley. He accused Farley of being illiterate and of being inadequate not only as a Congressman but as a bartender, too.

Farley won, but only by a slim margin of seventeen hundred. In preceding years, Tammany had won elections by as many as sixteen thousand votes. Thousands of people had voted for La Guardia, who emerged from his defeat more dangerous than any opponent of Tammany had ever been in the Fourteenth Congressional District.

In the Republican Party's book, the name of Fiorello La Guardia was becoming easier to spell. To keep the young lawyer where they could put their hands on him politically, the Republican leaders had him appointed a Deputy Attorney General of the State of New York, in New York City. This was not too difficult to accomplish because Harry Andrews, who helped to manage Fiorello's campaign, was secretary to State Republican Committee Chairman Frederick Tanner. And Tanner was helping Charles S. Whitman, newly-elected Republican Governor, decide on the appointments of new officials.

"If you watch your step, F.H.," said Espresso, "you're gonna be a big man around here."

Fiorello laughed. "Yeah, I know. Tanner might need me for 1916. That's okay. I might need him, too."

Fiorello tackled his new job with gusto. From the office of Weil, La Guardia & Espen, a law firm which he had joined a year earlier, he brought along his blonde, blue-eyed, twenty-year-old secretary, Marie Fischer. In their brief association, he had begun to find her indispensable. Her intelligence and ability did not desert her when he loaded her with work or when he lost his temper, both of which happened frequently. In short, she understood him.

In the spirit of Sheriff Bucky O'Neill, Fiorello was gleefully determined to visit justice on all the corporate evildoers he could find skulking in the dark corners of his jurisdiction. But it wasn't simple. He discovered, to his disgust, that his superiors didn't want him to work too hard at winning certain cases whose records he had found gathering dust in the office files. His suit against Long Island oyster companies for dredging underage scallops was thrown out of court because lawyers for the defense had the State law changed before Fiorello could force the case to trial. He was roundly reprimanded for filing a complaint against nearby New Jersey factories whose fumes polluted New York air. Who was he, his superiors wanted to know, to initiate an action in the United States Supreme Court without asking their permission?

The worst blow to La Guardia was the decision in the case he initiated against meat packers for misstating the weights of their hams and bacons on the paper wrappers. State Senator James J. Walker, one of Tammany's most promising young men, was attorney for the packers. Senator Walker explained to the court

that the Weights and Measures Law, which La Guardia was trying to enforce, applied only to meat sold in containers and not in
paper wrappers. The Senator was absolutely certain about the
intention of the law, he assured the court, because he was himself
the author of it. . . . "Case dismissed!"

The two antagonists had been acquaintances for some time.
They left the courtroom together and Fiorello accepted the af-
fable Jimmy's invitation to join him and the judge at a nearby
café.

"Jimmy," said the defeated lawyer, "a lot of little storekeep-
ers have been fined for selling those paper-wrapped hams."

"Stop worrying," said the Senator.

"How can you go into court to defeat your own law?" Fiorello protested.

"When are you going to get wise?" Jimmy smiled. "Are you
in politics for love?"

Actually, La Guardia had little time for such light acquaintances as Jimmy Walker. But Fiorello was no hermit. He relished comradeship and the swift give and take of bright talk with
good friends. Among his intimates of the period were Raimondo
Canudo, Italian-born lawyer and editor of *Sicilia*, a weekly newspaper for immigrant readers; August Bellanca, frail organizer for
the Amalgamated Clothing Workers; his brother, Giusseppe, a
pioneering aeronautical designer; and Antonio Calitri, a poet.
The circle also included Arturo Giovannitti, a poet who was also
a labor organizer; Giovanni Fabrizio, a flutist in the New York
Philharmonic; Onorio Ruotolo, painter, sculptor, poet, and editor of a little magazine of the arts called *Il Fuoco* (The Flame);
Attilio Piccirilli, the sculptor whose monument to *The Maine*
was unveiled in Columbus Circle in 1913.

Love did not overtake Fiorello until he met twenty-one-
year-old Thea Almerigotti in 1915. Fiorello had noticed her from
the far end of the table in Duenicci's *penzione* (boarding house)
where they both took their evening meals.

"You come from the north of Italy, don't you?" he asked.

The golden-haired girl, who towered inches above him replied, "I was born in Trieste."

Fiorello's enchantment was complete. "Trieste is my mother's city," he exclaimed. "Did you know any Luzzatos or Coens in Trieste? That's my mother's family. Prime Minister Luigi Luzzato was a distant relative . . ." he stopped in mid-sentence, made aware by her sympathetic smile that he needn't try so hard. They talked about other things and learned from each other that he had a flat at 39 Charles Street and that she lived in a furnished room on Bank Street nearby; that she was a dress designer and that he was a lawyer (as if she didn't know); that she was a Catholic and that he was a member of Garibaldi Lodge No. 542 of the Masons, but that Father Demo, pastor of the Church of Our Lady of Pompei was a friend of his.

On their first Sunday afternoon date, they took a trolley ride up Broadway to Central Park and Fiorello showed her Piccirilli's memorial to *The Maine*. As they strolled through the park, they exchanged confidences.

This was the beginning of a long courtship in which Thea stood by patiently as Fiorello plunged into the tumult of the 1916 Congressional election. With Andrews and Espresso he attended dances, *bar mitzvahs*, fraternal society meetings, and other gatherings.

When Fiorello found out that Hamilton Fish, Jr., a rich outsider from Putnam County, wanted the nomination in return for a contribution to the party treasury, Fiorello was furious. "I'm going to run for Congress from this district in November," he told State Chairman Tanner. "If you put up anybody else, I'll run against him in the primary election." Tanner yielded. Fiorello was nominated, unopposed, and found himself in a return engagement against Mike Farley, who was running for re-election.

This time Fiorello didn't wait for a starting signal from the organization. In another Ford, with more signs, he began an endless round of speeches at street corners. The war in Europe was two years old and mild interest had given way to high emotions in the Fourteenth Congressional District. In Yiddish speeches, he predicted the overthrow of the hated Czar Nicholas II. In the Irish districts, he let the voters know he was a well-wisher of the Irish Republican Army. He had no difficulty in revealing his opinions about the war to any immigrant group except the Germans. Some immigrants wished only for disaster to the rulers of the countries from which they came.

Among the Germans who didn't particularly love Kaiser Wilhelm, but who wouldn't want to see the Fatherland lose a war, he had the support of the Ridder brothers' *Staats-Zeitung*, an influential German-language newspaper. He indicated to them that he was not in sympathy with the growing anti-German feeling in the United States. As a result, they published editorials and made speeches urging his election.

Fiorello carried the fight to Farley. He questioned the saloonkeeper's reputation, and, from a truck parked in front of the saloon, he challenged his opponent to come out and debate the issues. Farley was embarrassed. He wasn't familiar with the issues in his own district, to say nothing of national issues. He stayed behind his bar and tried to ignore his cocky young opponent.

In Tammany strongholds truth was not all-powerful. It was often overcome by fists. But the La Guardia campaign committee had young supporters whose fists were as hard as Tammany's. On election day La Guardia and his poll watchers succeeded in enforcing a fairly honest count. In the toughest election district, he took pains to put the Democratic boss, Charlie Culkin, on notice that he would not tolerate any ballot stealing.

When he and Espresso had checked their last ballot box that night, Fiorello knew he had won. He was going to Congress! He had polled 7,272 votes, 357 more than Farley. The margin was small but the victory was big. He was the first Republican to be elected to Congress from his district. With his black, broad-brimmed Western-style hat pushed back at a jubilant angle, Fiorello sauntered into the headquarters of the Twenty-Fifth A.D. Republican Club expecting an ovation suitable to the occasion, but the few hard core hangers-on who had remained turned stony faces toward him and Louis. From the back room he could hear a fellow club member arguing with the Democratic leader of the district, "No, Joe, we didn't double-cross you. We didn't do anything for him. You just can't control La Guardia." The function-

ary spoke more truly than he knew. La Guardia was on his way
to becoming the most uncontrollable Republican with which the
Grand Old Party had ever been blessed and burdened.

Fiorello was also unmanageable as a suitor. He took it for
granted that Thea would understand the necessity of combining
courtship and politics. She did, and permitted herself to be swept
into the orbit of his campaign activities—applauding him at
meetings, attending other people's weddings, and shaking hands
with voters at funerals. This was no ordinary man who had
sought her out. She knew that the courting was going to be done
on his terms. There were no two ways about it; she was in love
with him. And now he was going to Washington to be a Congressman, without her. She understood that he would not permit
anything to distract him from the role he had dreamed of so
long. She could forget him or wait for him. She decided to wait.

CHAPTER 9

He Wanted Wings

THE ELMS ALONG THE WIDE AVENUES WERE FLOWERING
pale green and the forsythia hedges were shining a golden glow.
In the gracious park near the Capitol, even the stone statues of
otherwise forgotten heroes took on a touch of vitality in spring.

Two men in Washington, D. C., that morning of April 2,
1917, were indifferent to the promise of the new season. Woodrow Wilson, President of the United States, had spent a sleepless
night over the frightful decision he was to ask of the nation that
same evening. Fiorello La Guardia, freshman in the House of
Representatives, walked in the early morning chill oppressed by
doubts of himself and by misgivings of the future.

Always irrepressible and, before this, always as big as the
occasion confronting him, he suddenly felt small. His wide-
brimmed hat settled lower and lower on his brow as he walked
the deserted park paths, thinking, thinking. This was to be the
first time a son of Italian immigrants would take a seat in Congress. One false move and eager unfriendly critics would say,
"Well, what can you expect of that chesty little wop?"

In Washington, he would be under the eye of tough, experi-
enced colleagues, especially because of his astonishing election
triumph over Tammany. At home he was fair game for his defeated opponents, for the newspapers, and for every voter. It was

59

meant to be so; it was right for the people to call elected officials to account for their conduct in office.

If it weren't for the war in Europe and the repeated sinking of American merchant ships with heavy loss of life by German submarines, he wouldn't be in Washington this morning. Wilson had called the Sixty-Fifth Congress into extraordinary session for a purpose of which the whole world was aware—a declaration of war on Germany.

Plodding through the park, Fiorello pondered the question of how he could be true both to himself and his constituents. Many of the voters back home did not want war. Nor could he ignore the arguments of Wisconsin's Senator Robert La Follette and others that the United States was being dragged into the conflict to protect the loans which American bankers had made to England, France, and Russia. Fiorello knew that business interests were avid for the profits to be made from equipping an army and transporting it overseas. Also, he could not resist the tide of American anger against Germany without being accused of disloyalty. Moreover, his own feelings and opinions urged him to vote for war. He believed that German rule in Europe was a menace to world democracy. The logic and morality of Teddy Roosevelt's "Square Deal" and Woodrow Wilson's "New Freedom" had left the United States no choice except the battlefields of France.

By the time he entered the House building at noon, he had a good idea of what he would do. He walked down the aisle to his desk, eyes front, chest out, like a Whipple Barracks officer on parade. His sense of the importance of the occasion was heightened by the names that resounded through the chamber as the clerk read the roll: "Arizona—Carl Hayden . . ." A pang of yearning for his boyhood, for the sun and the mountains, for Achille and the bugler blowing retreat, caused Fiorello to scan the room for a sight of the man who answered "present." Other names crowded into his attention—Tom Connally of Texas, James Byrnes of South Carolina, Cordell Hull of Tennessee, Champ Clark of Missouri, James Mann of Illinois, and wonder of wonders, the first woman Representative, Jeannette Rankin of Montana.

The rest of the afternoon was taken up with the election of officers. The principal contest was for Speaker of the House.

After a forty-three-minute recess from its separate deliberations of the day, House and Senate convened in joint session at 8:30 P.M. "to receive a communication concerning grave matters of national policy." President Wilson, re-elected a few months earlier on the slogan, "He kept us out of war," came to the Capitol under armed cavalry escort to fend off the embarrassment of a pacifist demonstration.

Looking from the rostrum at this assembly of the Congress, the Supreme Court, the Cabinet, the foreign diplomatic corps, Wilson began to read the most portentous words America had heard since the attack on Fort Sumter:

"The present German submarine warfare against commerce is warfare against mankind . . . American ships have been sunk, American lives have been taken . . . but the ships and people of other neutral and friendly nations have been sunk and overwhelmed in the waters in the same way. The challenge is to all mankind . . .

"We are glad . . . to fight thus for the ultimate peace of the world and for the liberation of its peoples, the German people included; for the rights of nations, great and small, and the privilege of men everywhere to choose their way of life and of obedience. The world must be made safe for democracy. Its peace must be planted upon the tested foundations of political liberty." Somberly, he continued, "It is a fearful thing to lead this great, peaceful nation into war . . ."

The issue was debated fervently and bitterly in House and Senate for three days and past midnight into a fourth. When the tally was taken shortly after 3:00 A.M. on Good Friday, April 6, Fiorello voted with the 372 other Representatives who favored a declaration of war. Nonetheless, he could only admire Congresswoman Rankin when she rose, unhappy but resolute, and said, "I want to stand by my country, but I cannot vote for war."

Traditionally, freshman Congressmen are seen and not heard. In the Sixty-Fifth Congress, the close division between Democrats and Republicans gave the voices and votes of new members an importance that made it easier for Fiorello to violate

the custom. He felt no need to serve an "apprenticeship." He
spoke up to and with his elders in the House whenever he
thought it necessary.

On April 3, he introduced House Resolution 345 "making
the fraudulent sale of war materials a felony punishable by im-
prisonment in time of peace and by death in time of war." In
proposing this Act of Congress, he wanted not so much to
avenge his father's shattering illness in the military pesthole of
Tampa, as to prevent the deaths of other people for the enrich-
ment of the few.

Irene would have understood her son's legislative ferocity . . . The year before his election she had visited him and
found a mother's gratification in his prosperity, his promising
future, and in their warm relationship. Then she had gone back
to Budapest to live out her few remaining months with Gemma
and her husband.

To Thea, whom he thought of often and tenderly when his
mind wasn't otherwise occupied, he wrote:

"My bill was referred to the Committee on the Judiciary.
Which is another way of saying it will be buried there. But I had
to get it off my chest. Something has to be done so that lives
are not traded for money. I'll have to try again." He never got
around to it. The Congressional calendar was crammed with bills
pertaining to the conduct of the war. Studiously, the thirty-four-
year-old lawmaker examined every measure that reached his
desk. Each bill had to answer three questions: would it help win
the war; would it make a fair division of the war's economic burdens among rich and poor; would it endanger democracy at
home in the name of defending it overseas?

He supported the Liberty Loan Bill to raise war funds by
public subscription, but opposed a provision which would have
given profiteering advantages to big-money investors.

On the War Revenue Bill, the largest tax proposal which
had ever confronted Congress, La Guardia argued for higher ex-
emptions for wage earners and against the "war tax" on candy
selling for less than thirty cents a package. This candy was usually bought by the children of low-income families. He failed in
both instances, but he succeeded in adding a ten per cent tax on

the more expensive seats at the opera and other places of amusement.

La Guardia favored the Lever Food and Fuel Control Act giving the Federal Government wartime power to control the production and distribution of food and other essential items. He offered an amendment, which was defeated, authorizing the same kind of government controls in peacetime, too. The framers of the Constitution, he argued, did not imagine that there would ever be a day when the nation's necessities of life could be monopolized. Otherwise, he assured the House, they would have listed food, clothing, and shelter among man's inalienable rights.

As enthusiastic as he was for this war, he was opposed to the Espionage Act, which placed any American who opposed the war or criticized the way it was conducted in the same class as an enemy spy. He spoke at length against the bill, objecting particularly to Section Four which could have been used to prevent legitimate protests against price gouging, contract frauds, or inefficiency in government departments in connection with the war effort.

"The people of this country are united in their demand that the scandals, abuses, graft, and incompetency of 1898 will not be repeated," he stormed on the floor of the House. "The press is their medium of detecting and exposing these abuses and crimes. It is our duty to do nothing which will impair, restrict, or limit the press in the fulfillment of that duty . . . We have the responsibility of carrying this country through this war without impairing or limiting any of her institutions of true liberty . . ." The bill was passed but he voted against it, even though the section to which he objected most was struck out.

There was no such doubt in his mind about the Selective Service Act for drafting men into the armed forces, even though he was well aware that many of the voters in his district didn't like the idea. In a letter to his constituency he wrote:

"I think conscription is needed and I am trying to educate the people up to it. There have been attempts to introduce bills in Congress which would exempt the farmer from service, or the cotton grower, or the tobacco grower. If New York doesn't watch out she will be having to supply as large a proportion of the Army as she now does of the taxes, which is one third. The only way to avoid this is to institute compulsory service. It is up to you to respond; don't blame me if you don't like the way I vote."

To re-enforce this warning, La Guardia shuttled between Washington and New York to make fiery speeches in his district urging support for the war and for the draft measure.

In the final days of the heated debate, an angry Congressman who opposed the bill flung the ultimate challenge at his colleagues: "How many gentlemen who are so eager to send our youth to war in a foreign country will stand up and say *they* are ready to go, too?"

With neither haste nor hesitation, Fiorello stood up. The hall was stilled as everyone looked about the chamber to see who else was standing. There were four others: Haskell of Brooklyn, Heintz of Ohio, Gardner of Massachusetts, and Johnson of South Dakota. The bill was passed by the House on April 28. It became a law on May 18.

Thea Almerigotti was not altogether surprised about Fiorello's decision to enlist. She made a brave show of sympathy and understanding as thousands of other women were doing that year. She did see clearly that her remarkable fiancé was happier since his election to Congress than she had ever known him to be.

"Fiorello," she once said to him in jest, "I think you like being a papa to all the people of your district and in the whole United States."

"You are right, *cara mia*," he replied with more earnestness than she had expected. "Everybody has representatives in Washington, except the people. That's what I'm there for."

"Then why are you joining the Army?"

"Because I promised I would not vote for the draft unless I joined the Army myself."

"Did you *have* to vote for the draft?"

"Listen, Thea, I'm going to make a promise to you, too. When I come back from Europe, Trieste will be free. It will be part of Italy again. I'll tend to it personally."

Thea laughed. "I'll miss you, Fiorello. Nobody else makes me such great promises."

"Now wait a minute, I'm not going yet."

In mid-July he enlisted in the Aviation Section of the Signal Corps. He was made a first lieutenant, not because he was a Congressman but because he knew how to fly, as flying went in those days. His interest in aviation dated back to the years when he first met the Bellanca brothers. In Giusseppe's little flying school on Long Island, Fiorello had learned to get a small, thirty-horsepower monoplane off the ground and set it down again with little or no damage to plane or pilot. In return, he taught Bellanca how to drive a Model T Ford and did free legal work for his aircraft manufacturing company.

In the ten weeks following his enlistment, Fiorello became the hero of New York's Italian population. He addressed war rallies, and was made much of both by the big daily newspapers and the Italian-language press. His triumphal return to Greenwich Village inevitably included a visit with Chich Giordano. They talked:

"I'm taking 156 aviation cadets to Foggia in a few weeks."

"I want to go with you, Fiorello."

"How can you? You're married, you're over-age, you've got three children and a barber shop!"

"I've got flat feet, too. What good is it to have a Congressman for a friend if he can't get me into the Army?"

"You're crazy."

"We will see who's crazy. Find a way."

Fiorello found a way by pulling a few wires and getting Chich assigned to his outfit as cook and orderly. The meals were unattractive but everyone had good haircuts.

La Guardia's cadets were a rather elite crew, college-educated, upper-class young men of affairs. The most distinguished was Albert Spalding, famous as a concert violinist, who was assigned to the unit because he knew the Italian language. By mid-October, 1917, the outfit was settled in Foggia, Achille La Guardia's birthplace, under the command of Major (later Major General) William Ord Ryan. Fiorello, in charge of West Camp, looked after his men as lovingly and sternly as he looked after the emigrants when he was a consular officer. He learned to fly the big clumsy Caproni bombers, went on bombing missions over the Austrian front, survived a crash, and conducted a running feud with Major Ryan. Eventually A.E.F. headquarters told Ryan, as gently as possible, that he would have to defer to his subordinate officer's decisions on almost everything. This may have been due, in part, to the fact that Fiorello did not hesitate to remind the military authorities that he was a Congressman as well as a mere Army captain.

In any event, it became quickly apparent to the American high command in Paris and to the Italian government in Rome that confining Fiorello to the official limits of an Army captain's authority was as wasteful as using a locomotive to pull a hay cart. They soon began to make wider use of his executive abilities. He shuttled between the capitals on special missions, wrote reports on political conditions in Italy, and went to Barcelona to liberate a million and a half dollars' worth of raw materials from an embargo which noncombatant Spain had decreed to appease the Germans. In co-operation with U. S. Army Intelligence, he worked on a plot for starting a revolution in Hungary, until the undertaking was vetoed by President Wilson. In the course of these special duties, he met General Pershing, King Victor Emmanuel, members of the Italian cabinet, and important American officials.

Italy had entered the conflict reluctantly and had fought it the same way. Disheartened by the loss of 300,000 men and vast stores of war materials at Caporetto, the Italian people were sick of the war and of being neglected by their allies. To keep Italy fighting, a swift and sweeping reversal of public opinion was needed. U. S. Ambassador Thomas Nelson Page chose La Guardia to launch a propaganda effort. His ancestry, his ability to speak Italian, his knowledge of Central European affairs, and his willingness to risk an embarrassing failure, made Fiorello just right for the job.

The understanding was that if Fiorello's first public speech in Genoa was a failure, the Ambassador would tell the world that Captain La Guardia was not speaking for his Government. The Genoa meeting was a huge success. This was not some stiff, foreign brass hat speaking condescendingly to the Italian people. This short, dark man, his voice rising, shrilling, and falling in angry, loving, pleading coloratura, was one of their own. More important, he seemed to know what he was talking about. In rapid succession, with Albert Spalding as his aide, Fiorello spoke in Naples, Rome, Milan, Bologna, Turin, Florence, and Bari. Confidently, Fiorello promised the Italian people a better life and a better world after Germany was defeated. He believed it.

CHAPTER 10

So This Is City Hall!

FOR HIS BELIEF THAT THE WAR COULD REALLY INSURE world democracy, Fiorello had to answer to a critical and unhappy constituency. Up for re-election, he returned to the United States with Army permission on October 28, 1918, wearing a major's leaves and three Italian medals. His name had been placed on the ballot while he was still overseas being shot at by Austrian antiaircraft gunners. There was only one week left before election day, but his war record, trumpeted by his supporters and the newspapers, had campaigned for him effectively in his absence.

A strange thing had happened. Major La Guardia, sworn enemy of Tammany, was running with Tammany's blessing. The Democrats had joined with the Republicans to support a Fusion ticket, not out of love for Fiorello but out of fear that a Socialist might walk off with the election. This was a frightening but real possibility to them. The Democrats and Republicans were equally disturbed by the prospect of a Socialist victory. The man to beat was Scott Nearing, a former University of Pennsylvania economics professor who had been jailed under an Espionage Act indictment for antiwar activities, which included writing a pamphlet called *The Great Madness*.

The United States had sent more than 2,000,000 troops to Europe; 106,516 men died in the trenches, behind the lines, or in training. More than 23,000 others had been permanently disabled. In civilian life, however, the war had produced some 17,000 new American millionaires. In the same period, the cost of living had doubled while wages had lagged painfully behind. Now, disenchantment and discontent were spreading among many segments of the nation's wage earners, including the newly returned veterans. In La Guardia's district, and in at least three others, the Socialists had an excellent chance of sending their candidates to Congress.

The returning war hero was keenly aware that he could lose votes instead of gaining them if he did nothing but harp on Nearing's antiwar activities. "The question of patriotism must not be introduced into this campaign," he said. "Scott Nearing must have a fighting chance."

After this fair statement, Fiorello proceeded to make his own accusations against Nearing and the other Socialists. He pictured their opposition to the war as a disservice and an injury to the common man. During the few days before the election, he stormed through his district making speeches in which he represented himself as a better defender of the people's interests than the Socialists. "I am against war," he cried in a debate with Nearing, "and because I am against war I *went* to war, to fight against war."

Hammering away in his riveting gun delivery, he pointed out that European Socialists, in every country, had supported the warring governments of their homelands. For American Socialists to oppose their own country's participation in the war, he asserted, was the same as supporting the Kaiser's imperialism.

In the Twentieth Congressional District, embracing Italian- and Jewish-populated East Harlem, Fiorello spoke for the Fusion candidacy of Isaac Siegel and launched bitter attacks against the Socialist candidate. "I charge Morris Hillquit with being a tool and an ally of the Kaiser," he shouted. But he lost no opportunity to let the voters know that he sympathized with their immediate problems.

At outdoor rallies, he chanted a litany of wage-earners' grievances: "You paid nine cents a quart for milk before the war, now you pay fifteen. Eggs used to be thirty-seven cents a dozen.

Now they are sixty-two cents. The price of meat and butter has doubled. Sure, you're getting a little more money than you used to get but your real wages have been cut in two. A dollar today buys less than half of what it bought in 1914." He wanted to go back to Congress, he told the voters, to improve their lot in life *now* without waiting for Socialism. That would take too long, he warned.

The voters responded. Fiorello won his second term in the House with 14,523 votes against Nearing's 6,214. He had also helped Congressman Siegel keep his seat in the Twentieth. A week after Fiorello's election victory came the military victory of the Allies over Germany. Major La Guardia resigned his commission, though he cherished the title ever after. He attended the final session of the Sixty-Fifth Congress, to complete his freshman term. Congress returned the compliment by voting him his back pay which had been held in abeyance during his Army service.

Quick as he was to make life-and-death decisions in war and in politics there was one decision he had postponed for a long time but could put off no longer. What was to become of him and Thea Almerigotti? He was thirty-six years old, a man of substantial political reputation and promising future. Thea was twenty-four. She had shown her devotion by fending off other suitors and waiting for him through a war and two election campaigns.

They were married in the rectory of St. Patrick's Cathedral on March 4, 1919. There was a wedding breakfast at the Netherlands Hotel and a honeymoon trip. They took up residence in Fiorello's four-room flat at 39 Charles Street. Life promised to be wonderful. They went to hear Italian operas, spent evenings with Fiorello's colorful friends, and socialized occasionally with some of his political colleagues. Thea, however, was often alone because her husband was first and foremost a Congressman. He was in Washington, he was at Republican organization meetings, he was everywhere. She cherished him but she must have smiled at the newspaper story which first called public attention to the fact that her husband's first name meant "Little Flower." If there was anything floral about Fiorello, it could only be his resem-

blance to those dark, durable wrought-iron blooms that adorned
the grillwork on the porches of the older private homes in Greenwich Village.

The year 1919 was the year an era ended. It was a year of
mourning for the deaths of dynasties and jubilation over the rise
of new governments, or vice versa, depending on which side one
was on. The Hohenzollerns and the Hapsburgs had lost their
thrones, the Romanoffs their heads. But there was still truth in
the saying that the sun never sets on the British Empire.

The sun was certainly setting on President Wilson's crusade
to teach the rulers of Europe that they must be guided by moral
principles instead of their lust for power. His proposals for a just,
unvengeful peace were negotiated to death at the Paris Conference and his plea for American participation in a League of Nations to prevent future wars was maneuvered, debated, and voted
to death in the Senate. On both sides of the Atlantic, he had failed
in his dedicated struggle.

The defeat of the Wilsonian ideal closed the three decades
of liberalism in which Fiorello had grown up. The Populism of
Bucky O'Neill and Jacob Coxey during the 1890's had expressed
the resistance of the people to being exploited by the railroads,
the industrial trusts, and the big banking houses. The Democrats,
under Bryan's leadership, had seized the Populist banner. The
Square Deal of Teddy Roosevelt and the New Freedom of
Woodrow Wilson, which were, after all, not very far apart, had
been attempts to allay the discontent of the workingmen by putting restraints on the privileges of the wealthy. Now the path of
American liberalism had meandered into the middle of a political
nowhere. Fiorello, being a man of action rather than a theorist,
began to play rugged politics on behalf of the wage earner, the
small businessman, the ordinary American, whether native or foreign born.

Two wars had come and gone. They had aroused his sweeping, all-out patriotism. They had also churned up his indignation
at the special advantages of the rich and the special burdens of
the poor, in war as well as in peace. In his second Congressional
term he found ample scope for these feelings which dominated
his politics and personality. He helped cut the Wilson administra-

tion's proposed peacetime army of half a million men to 200,000, but he introduced a bill to spend fifteen million dollars to build up an air force, while attacking the waste of earlier aviation funds. He stormed against the profiteers who were having a field day with the huge stockpiles of surplus war materials, demanded the reinstatement of veterans in their prewar jobs, and cried out for an end to high food prices, war taxes, and rent-gouging. He campaigned for the annexation of Fiume to Italy and protested against anti-Semitism in Central Europe.

The Congressman gave stout support to President Wilson's fight for American participation in the League of Nations. He favored a "treat 'em rough" policy against the I.W.W. (International Workers of the World, whose tactics he did not like), but introduced a resolution for the repeal of the Espionage Act because of its oppressive effects on civil liberties.

He fell into natural alignment with the anti-Prohibition bloc and quickly became one of its most aggressive spokesmen in House debates on the Volstead Act which was to become the principal means of enforcing the Prohibition Amendment. He was aroused not only by the impracticality of the law but by the argument of its advocates that prohibition was needed to control the dissolute and generally objectionable behavior of "the lower classes" and "the foreign elements" in the big cities. More than one Representative from the "dry" regions of the South and Midwest felt the lash of his cosmopolitan wit.

By instinct, he shied away from the discipline of his own party without moving closer to the opposition. Sometimes he made speeches and proposals which alarmed both sides of the House, but his insurgent conduct was reassuring to the voters of the Fourteenth Congressional District and gratifying to most of New York's foreign-born population.

Late in the summer of 1919, Sam Koenig, Republican County Chairman in Manhattan, summoned Fiorello to a private conference. The subject was the special fall election for president of the New York City Board of Aldermen, to fill the post left vacant by the election of Alfred E. Smith as governor of New York State.

"We want you to run for Al Smith's job," said Koenig.

"Now just a minute, Sam . . ." Fiorello protested.

"If you win, you get the Party's nomination for mayor in 1921."

"I like being in Congress, Sam."

"Fiorello," sighed Koenig, "it's not so much a matter of what you like as it is of what the Party needs. Tammany doesn't have another Al Smith right now and the voters like you, Fiorello."

"And if I lose?"

"You've still got your seat in Congress. Besides, you're young and you've got a future."

Fiorello's imagination was fired. To beat Tammany, to drive out the payroll parasites and the loafers, to clean the municipal household from top to bottom with a merciless broom . . . what a challenge!

"Sam," he said, "I need a little time to think about it."

At home, he thought about it out loud, with Thea as his audience:

"They need me, sweetheart, and I need them. Sure I want to be mayor. Do you know what a good mayor could do for New York City?"

"I think so."

"I'll tell you. New York is the biggest and richest city in the world. A good mayor could also make it a wonderful town to live in. The streets are filthy, the schools overcrowded, the hospitals run down, and the jails aren't fit even for criminals. I could change all that. There's money enough, but it's chiseled and wasted away by crooks and incompetents. Why shouldn't the city put some of that money into decent apartment buildings so we could tear down a lot of these miserable old slums? And how about the landlords all over town? It's time somebody went up to Albany and raised hell about them. Thea, sweetheart, I'm going to take that nomination!"

Thea smiled, more out of personal satisfaction than political enthusiasm. She was pregnant and welcomed the possibility that her husband might hold municipal office. If he were elected they would be separated only by the distance between City Hall and their Charles Street flat instead of by the two hundred miles be-

tween New York and Washington, during Congressional sessions.
When the newspapermen asked him about Koenig's offer, Fiorello answered with characteristic cockiness: "I can do good work in Congress and I believe I have done and am doing good work but, of course, if I am nominated, I will have to make the race—and I will win!" The newsmen enjoyed interviewing this explosive little man. He was what they called "good copy." He might be a trifle pompous on occasion but he was never dull. He was colorful, straightforward, quotable.

There was more than cockiness in his statements to the press. He sensed, sooner than most, the coming change of political seasons which would favor him locally, just as it would favor the Republican Party nationally in the 1920 election. When that time came, the virtual collapse of the Wilson administration made an easy victory possible for presidential candidate Warren G. Harding, and his running mate, Calvin Coolidge. Harding was an undistinguished Senator from Ohio; Coolidge was the colorless Governor of Massachusetts who achieved national prominence late in 1919 by breaking a strike of the newly formed Boston policemen's union. As contenders against this team the Democrats chose Ohio's Governor James M. Cox, who was handicapped by his identification with Wilson's policies, and the politically untried Franklin D. Roosevelt, Wilson's wartime Assistant Secretary of the Navy.

La Guardia went into the race with his customary zest. He won by a small margin, 1,530 votes. It was enough, however, to give New York two years of unaccustomed drama in municipal affairs, some of it resembling a serialized barroom brawl. As President of the Board of Aldermen, La Guardia was second-ranking executive of the City of New York. He had three votes in the Board of Estimate and Apportionment, the city's "executive committee," he was Acting Mayor in the absence of John F. Hylan, and he presided at the aldermanic meetings, in which he could not vote, except in case of a tie. But the parliamentary law governing the Board did permit him to talk. It was a good law, very much like the one which permits Niagara Falls to continue falling. He made the most of it.

The Little Flower took office on January 1, 1920. As he en-

tered the City Hall, he paused in the spacious rotunda, glanced
admiringly at the superbly curved marble staircase, and looked
around to get his bearings. The Mayor's wing was to the left. His
own office was to the right. For the moment, he turned right.

With the indispensable Marie Fischer as adjutant, Fiorello
plunged into a program of executive activity and controversy
that rattled the window panes of City Hall. Spreading farther,
the shock waves also produced an enthusiastic rattling of typewriters in the newspaper offices just across the street from City
Hall Park.

Before his first month in office was over, he addressed public meetings, protesting against the State Legislature's efforts to
expel five Socialist assemblymen who had been elected in November. In the Board of Aldermen he blocked efforts to unseat
four Socialists who had been elected to that body.

"In ousting the five Socialist assemblymen," La Guardia said,
"a dangerous precedent has been created. If we deprive the
Socialists of their legal rights after legitimate use of the ballot;
if we deprive them of free speech and of the free press, they will
be compelled to resort to the same sort of methods used in Russia . . . With grain, eggs, and oatmeal becoming luxuries in the
average family, these Socialists, along with the general public,
are right in demanding a radical change in conditions."

His efforts to prevent inefficiency and graft in the spending
of municipal funds plunged him into a spectacular battle with
Comptroller Charles L. Craig, third-ranking elected city official.
Personality as well as politics made natural antagonists of these
two. The fact that the Comptroller was the law partner of
James A. Foley, son-in-law of Charlie Murphy, the big
Tammany boss, added an extra dash to all La Guardia-Craig ex-
plosions.

He discovered Craig had approved contracts which guaranteed fantastic prices for the materials and construction work on
a new county courthouse. With the support of his Republican
colleague, Manhattan Borough President Henry H. Curran, La
Guardia persuaded Mayor Hylan, a Democrat, to cancel the contracts and order an investigation. Dozens of grand jury indict-
ments were handed down and the chief offenders went to the

State penitentiary. Craig's connection with the contracts, while highly unethical, was apparently not illegal. As a Tammany man, he had just been doing what came naturally. Besides putting a damper on the exuberant Tammany grafting, Fiorello saved the city more than three million dollars.

The Little Flower also thwarted a Craig-sponsored schedule of salary increases which would have benefited political appointees in the high brackets at the expense of civil servants sorely in need of cost-of-living raises. With Mayor Hylan's backing he forced through a plan which excluded employees earning more than five thousand dollars a year.

In his spare time, he castigated Craig, his most convenient symbol for Tammany, as a front for the private companies which leased and operated the New York subways. Craig had approved a loan to one of the companies which was clamoring for legislation that endangered the pillar of New York's civic pride, the five-cent fare.

Having felt the lash of La Guardia's tongue for weeks, the victim hit back when he was accused of favoring personal friends in his conduct of city affairs. "The statement by the Aldermanic President," Craig roared, "is made from whole cloth with utter disregard of facts. It is the wildest kind of radical socialistic, blackguardia statement!"

The reporters scratched happily on their note pads, eagerly listening for the Little Flower's smashing retort. He was so astounded that he didn't have one. He could only say lamely, "The record speaks for itself."

In a decade called "the roaring twenties," La Guardia was one of the earliest, loudest, and most persistent roarers. At a public forum in the ultrarespectable Church of the Ascension, at Fifth Avenue and Tenth Street, he declared he would be in favor of a law to cut off the hand of a public official who accepted bribes.

"And I would also advocate cutting off both hands of the man who gave the bribe," he added. His listeners knew he didn't mean this literally, but they were shocked by the savageness of the statement.

Appearing in Albany at a legislative hearing on a rent control bill, La Guardia spread rage and consternation among the six hundred landlords who had come to oppose the measure. He said, "I come not to praise the landlord but to bury him!" Bedlam broke loose in the hearing chamber and La Guardia's utterance broke into the headlines.

Newspaper editors found that there was no keeping La Guardia out of print. And the Republican State leadership was beginning to suspect there was no keeping him in line. The Little Flower was rapidly becoming their big headache. A deep antagonism had sprung up between Governor Nathan L. Miller, elected in November, 1920, and the young Aldermanic President. Both were members of the Republican Party. The only other thing they had in common was membership in the human race. Fiorello was a preacher of change who had come from the world of poverty and war. The Governor was a well-contented man devoted to the cult of machine politics. He heard no voices and saw no visions beyond the boundaries of upstate New York. He was repeatedly irritated by the liberal deeds and speeches of this Manhattan maverick with the Italian name. But he developed a positively Herodian hankering for Fiorello's head as a result of their collision over two issues.

One issue was the direct primary law, which Miller wanted repealed. La Guardia took it on himself to raise a public fuss against the repeal act which was pending in the Legislature. The other was a bill for financial relief of the New York subway system which gave more control of New York City transit matters to the state than to the city itself. What was worse, it included no guarantee of retaining the five-cent fare. Fiorello failed to prevent either repeal of the direct primary law or the passage of the transit relief bill, despite a vigorous public speaking campaign before civic organizations and Republican clubs throughout the city.

"The day will come," he prophesied, "when city transportation will be taken away from private owners and will become city property." And it did.

Miller was outraged by the political embarrassments the fiery Fiorello was creating for him. He destroyed the Little Flower's chances for the Republican mayoral designation in the

November, 1921, election. Other influential Republicans followed the Governor's leadership. Even La Guardia's good friend, Sam Koenig, who in all good faith had talked him into giving up his seat in Congress, could no longer support him. By late spring, La Guardia's hopes of succeeding John F. Hylan as chief executive of the world's largest city had been firmly and fatally trampled. He had started his term as aldermanic president by turning to the right, but his destiny lay to the left.

CHAPTER 11

The Bad Years

ON NEW YEAR'S DAY, 1920, MAJOR FIORELLO H. LA Guardia, President of the Board of Aldermen and his wife, Thea, the pretty immigrant ex-dress designer, had that wonderful feeling of everything going their way. Political and social fortunes aside, they had each other, they were in love, and Thea was going to have a baby.

The happiness of the couple was something their intimates could sense just by walking into their flat, which they often did. The La Guardias enjoyed entertaining their personal friends, most of whom had nothing to do with City Hall or party politics. In addition to the Major's longstanding cronies, Attilio Piccirilli, Onorio Ruotolo, and the Bellanca brothers, they enjoyed close friendships with Albert Spalding and with one of the most famous of twentieth-century Italians, Enrico Caruso.

Chich Giordano had a special standing. He came and went without invitation or ceremony. He was no match in sophistication, talent, or intellect for the company that Fiorello and Thea usually kept. He was just a self-respecting immigrant barber of peasant origin who offered them his boundless admiration. They could do no less than return such unselfish friendship in full measure.

When there were social gatherings, Fiorello cooked the mussel soup and the pasta, and Thea poured the wine, Prohibition or not. Everyone talked, laughed, argued, or sang.

Thea's baby, a girl, was born in June, 1920. They named her Fioretta Thea, but the parents' joy turned quickly to misgiving, then to anxiety and, before the year had passed, to the ultimate sorrow.

Fioretta did not flourish as a healthy new infant should. And Thea was not recovering from childbirth with the normal rapidity. On the contrary, she continued to look more peaked as the weeks went by and she coughed alarmingly. Fioretta and Thea were both ill. The doctors examined and examined and then uttered a terrifying word—tuberculosis. In the 1920's, the medical profession could do little more about tuberculosis than it could do forty years later about cancer. The bacilli lived in the dark, damp, and dirty corners of big cities and made themselves at home in the bodies of the ill-housed, undernourished, and overworked. Thea's lungs and the baby's spine were affected.

In December, 1920, La Guardia uprooted himself from Greenwich Village and moved his wife and daughter to a house he bought in a sparsely settled area of the Bronx. He hoped they would benefit by the "better air." All through that winter of 1921, Thea cared for the baby despite her own illness. During the day, Fiorello fought the increasingly sharp battles of his public life with the extra ferocity of a man suffering from a deep private distraction. At night, he lived with the sense of disaster that haunted his household.

The baby died of tuberculous meningitis early in May, 1921. Fiorello endured the blow, as one must. Thea had neither the physical nor emotional stamina for it. By June she was in a sanatorium. It was there that Fiorello had to tell her, because she asked about his prospects in the fall campaign, that the party leaders had reneged on their promise to give him the Republican mayoral nomination.

Thea made a shrewd, bitter joke of the matter: "They don't want to nominate you because they're afraid you'll win." He smiled, but he kept his thoughts to himself. That was undoubtedly it—he had frightened the Republican leadership so thoroughly that they would rather take their chances of losing with Henry Curran than have a winner like La Guardia on their hands. Well, he wasn't finished yet. He would run against Curran in the primary. At worst, he would be defeated, but if he beat Curran and won the November election, he would have a new reservoir of power at his command to make some sweeping changes in the life of New York City.

The proposals in the platform on which he based his primary campaign reflected his experiences as Aldermanic President. He had learned a lot in two years:

"Better Transit for a Five-Cent Fare" meant cracking down on the subway operators instead of lending a sympathetic ear to their demands for more financial advantages.

"Direct Primaries for All Elective Offices" meant taking the nominations for public office out of the hands of political machines and letting each party's rank and file voters choose the candidates.

"Lower Gas, Electricity, and Telephone Rates" meant just that.

"Efficient Municipal Management" had an endless number and variety of meanings. Above all, it meant honesty and responsibility on the part of every official and employee.

"Better Housing Facilities with Lower Rents" projected the idea of municipally built housing at reasonable rents, which would serve as an example of what low-income families had a right to expect. In a way, public housing meant going into competition with private landlords who couldn't or wouldn't provide decent low-rent apartments as a matter of good business.

To achieve any substantial part of this platform would require countless political battles, which were the kind of battles La Guardia relished.

All over town and across the nation, there were events, signs, and portents that sharpened Fiorello's fighting mood. For a year or so after the Armistice, the factories that had worked day and night during the war were able to continue selling their products overseas because European industry was still badly disabled. Farmers did well because large quantities of foodstuffs were still being shipped abroad. During 1920, however, Europe's demand for American goods slacked off. Factories and mines started to slow down. Many shut their gates for a time. Farmers found themselves growing bigger crops than they could sell. Stores and warehouses remained full of goods few could buy. Jobs became scarce. By August, 1921, there were almost five million unemployed. Some twenty thousand firms went out of business that year. Struggles began between employers, who tried to maintain profits by cutting wages and making fewer men do more work, and workers, who wanted more money rather than less because wages had never caught up with wartime prices. During the years 1919, 1920, and 1921, there were strikes all over the United States involving some seven million workers in the steel, coal, railroad, meat packing, and a dozen other important industries.

Times were so bad that ex-servicemen began to clamor for immediate payment of a cash bonus which would not be legally due to them until many years later. Self-styled patriots moved to take jobs away from noncitizens and give them to demobilized soldiers. Immigrants who had lived in the United States for decades but who had never acquired citizenship were suddenly faced with the threat of unemployment.

After a heavy snowfall in the winter of 1921, Fiorello saw thousands of badly dressed men shivering in a block-long line in front of the Department of Street Cleaning waiting to be hired for a few hours of snow shoveling.

The newspapers reported that a group of wealthy women, the Sunrise Ball Society, was giving a dance at the smart Ambassador Hotel to finance free soap-and-water stations for homeless men. Many churches observed Unemployment Sundays in which congregations were urged to give work to jobless men.

In Boston, a mysterious self-appointed leader of the unemployed, called Mr. Zero, recruited a band of 150 men who were willing to become the human merchandise in a "slave auction" on Boston Common, because no one would hire them for wages. In La Guardia's old congressional district, the famous movie star, Eugene O'Brien, presided over the breadline at the door of St. Mark's Church to help arouse public compassion for the unemployed. How like the old Prescott days when Fiorello had read of similar charity events in the *New York World*!

From July to September, La Guardia stormed through the five boroughs campaigning for the Republican mayoral nomination. It grew more obvious from day to day that the odds were against him. He had no money and no organization. He made up for it the best he could with a furious energy generated by the combination of his public anxieties and his private anguish. (The doctors held out no hope for Thea.) When the vote was counted, Fiorello finished a bad second in a field of four, with 38,000 votes against Henry Curran's 103,000. The other two candidates had never shown any significant strength.

In the 1920 presidential election, Thea, in common with other American women, exercised the right to vote for the first time following the ratification of the Nineteenth Amendment. She and Fiorello were photographed by newspaper cameramen as they put their folded paper ballots into the big wooden box with the stout hasp and formidable lock (which gave no ironclad guarantee against vote stealing).

Thea died of pulmonary tuberculosis on November 29, 1921. There was no sense of resignation in Fiorello's grief, only outrage and despair. After the funeral, he turned again to his duties in City Hall but he treated them as duties and nothing more. His feud with Comptroller Craig continued of its own momentum.

Almost from the moment of Thea's death, Chich Giordano looked after Fiorello. For several weeks he came to the house early every morning bringing newspapers, which Fiorello read while Chich prepared breakfast. They ate together in silence. Once, when the generous Giordano came into the room to say good morning, Fiorello looked up and screamed at him savagely in Italian, "What devil sent you? Go away!" Chich turned away, despondent at his friend's grief. When he came back an hour later, Fiorello greeted him quietly as though he had not seen him that day. In mid-December, as his term in office was expiring, La Guardia sailed to Cuba with his friend, Piccirilli, for a vacation.

According to the experts in the clubhouses and newspaper offices, Major La Guardia was finished politically. He was through, just as surely as Franklin D. Roosevelt, who, that same summer, had almost died from infantile paralysis, then recovered, limp-legged and in a wheel chair.

The two men were born the same year. Both appeared on the political scene in 1910—Roosevelt as a Democratic State Senator from Dutchess County, La Guardia as a Republican activist in Greenwich Village. Both had seen wartime service and had made deservedly excellent reputations—one as Assistant Secretary of the Navy, the other as a Congressman and as a flier. Each had become an important standard bearer for his party— Roosevelt as candidate for vice-president in the 1920 election, La Guardia as successful contender for New York City's second highest office. Roosevelt, descendant of New York's early Dutch settlers, and La Guardia, the son of recent immigrants, came from opposite ends of the social spectrum, but they were close in their political opinions. They were the heirs of the aggressive prewar liberal tradition which had lost popular favor with the victory of Harding and Coolidge in 1920.

Unless he wants to rot slowly, a man either lives or dies. Fiorello chose to live. But scars remained. Fiorello could never forget the overcrowded tenements, the poverty, the undernourishment, and the unwholesomeness of life that made tuberculosis a common disease among the poor and a threat to the comfortable and well-to-do. In his view, his wife and baby had been destroyed by the indifference of a society which permitted such evils to flourish, just as his father had died because a govermment had permitted itself to buy tainted meat for its soldiers.

Fiorello recovered but never forgot.

In January, 1922, he was back in New York to resume his long-abandoned law practice which was now more prosperous than in prewar days. Mayor Hylan, the Democrat who disliked Tammany Hall, helped him to be appointed special counsel for the City of New York in a court action involving the Queens County Water Supply Company. His work resulted in reducing the company's claim against the city from eleven million to three and a half million dollars. His fee was substantial. He also represented the city in legal actions to convince the Federal Government to create a deep-water ship channel in Jamaica Bay. Fiorello had other financially rewarding clients, but the little people with big troubles and slender purses began to come to his office again. And that is how he wanted it to be.

Fiorello needed to work. Work kept him from thinking about Thea and the baby. He began to be himself again, to see his friends, and to think about a political comeback.

CHAPTER 12

La Guardia Rides Again

IF FIORELLO LA GUARDIA HAD BEEN NO MORE THAN A politician, his public life would have been at an end in 1922. Instead, it was merely getting under way.

Italian voters throughout the state were unhappy with their lowly position in Republican councils. They were alarmed and angered by the wave of prejudice against "foreigners" which followed World War I. They felt, together with other New Yorkers of foreign origin and humble economic status, that they needed vigorous spokesmen on the political scene. One result was the organization of a League of Italian-American Republican Clubs, an event which could hardly have happened without the Little Flower's conspicuous participation.

Among those who had solid respect for Fiorello's political abilities was William Randolph Hearst, founder of the powerful newspaper empire. They had common ground in their opposition to Tammany. Hearst invited La Guardia to write a series of articles for the *New York Evening Journal*.

Since they couldn't keep him out of politics, the Republican machine leaders decided to keep him in their camp by offering him the nomination for Congress in lower East Harlem where he had campaigned successfully for Isaac Siegel in 1918. The man from Arizona was ready to ride again.

The Twentieth Congressional District of New York consisted of one humanity-packed square mile running north and south from Ninety-Ninth to One Hundred Twentieth Streets and westward from the East River to Fifth Avenue. Its population of some 250,000 was mostly Italian and Jewish, with an increasing number of Negroes plus substantial pockets of Irish, Germans, and Puerto Ricans. Different though they were from each other in most respects, these had one thing in common—poverty.

La Guardia's campaign platform was something which his Socialist opponent, William Karlin, couldn't improve and which his Tammany adversary, Henry Frank, didn't dare to offer. It included a minimum wage law, old-age pensions, workmen's compensation, child-labor laws, abolition of injunctions in labor disputes, a soldiers' bonus, publicly-owned electric power companies, modification of the Volstead Act to permit the sale of light wines and beer, freedom of speech for minority political groups, and United States leadership to outlaw war. In the three decades that followed, many of the reforms La Guardia advocated in 1922 were accomplished in actions of Congress and numerous state legislatures.

In a sense, his campaign was a repetition of 1918. He was politely derogatory of his Socialist opponent. "Mr. Karlin," he said, "is a conservative running on a radical ticket. I am a radical running on a conservative ticket." His ferocity was aroused, however, by a circular accusing him of anti-Semitism. It was signed "The Jewish Committee," but it had Tammany's marks all over it.

Fiorello shrewdly invited Frank, who was Jewish, to a debate, "to be conducted . . . entirely in the Yiddish language," on the subject, "Who Is Best Qualified to Represent All the People of the Twentieth Congressional District." They never confronted each other because Frank couldn't speak a word of Yiddish, as Fiorello well knew when he deluged the Jewish neighborhoods with copies of the challenge.

The election was a close one. Republican ward heelers turned a few dishonest dollars by quietly urging their satellites to vote for the Democrat. Karlin, moreover, had a strong following. Fiorello squeaked in by 254 votes, while New Yorkers enjoyed the irony of hearing Tammany complain that the election had been stolen. What really disturbed the old-line politicians was the vigorous volunteer organization which had surged out of the lower East Harlem tenements in response to the Little Flower's forceful leadership.

During the campaign, the Major told to the voters, "I may as well tell you now that I don't fit in with the average so-called 'Republican' of the East. I am a Progressive."

The Progressive movement, led by Wisconsin's Senator Robert M. La Follette, was a coalition rather than a formal political party. It consisted of local and regional groups and individuals dissatisfied with the machine politics of the two major parties. It was particularly strong in the northern tier of the Middle West. In many parts of the country, there existed the same grievances that had attracted farmers to the Populist movement at the beginning of the century. In the big cities, the Progressives drew support from workers, small businessmen, and intellectuals. The spirit of the Progressives was expressed in La Follette's statement, "The supreme issue is the encroachment of the powerful few upon the rights of the many." La Guardia subscribed to this view with all his heart. It was this belief that had thrust him into public life and had kept him there against powerful odds.

La Guardia's first term as Representative from the Twentieth began on March 4, 1923, but the Sixty-Eighth Congress did not convene until December. He didn't waste the months of waiting. He organized a consumers' strike against the high prices of meat in Harlem. It became city-wide and brought prices down as much as ten cents a pound, which was a victory for the wives of wage earners whose family budgets depended on endless penny-counting. In Buffalo, he helped the Amalgamated Clothing Workers Union win recognition from local employers. Back in New York, he revitalized the tenants' associations for a successful fight to preserve the state rent control law.

By the time Congress convened, Fiorello, with John M. Nelson of Wisconsin and Ray O. Woodruff of Michigan, was a recognized leader of the twenty-three Progressives in the House.

From December to July, 1924, he worked at the bewildering and exhausting pace to which few of his associates besides

Marie Fischer ever became fully accustomed. He fought against the Reed-Johnson immigration bill, ultimately passed, which discriminated against immigrants of non-Anglo-Saxon origin. He denounced the Ku Klux Klan and Big Business as partners in a conspiracy to run the country. He lashed out bitterly at some of his colleagues who made speeches expressing their racial prejudice. He gave leadership in defeating the tax program of Andrew Mellon, millionaire Secretary of the Treasury, who proposed to abolish inheritance and excess profits taxes and to slash income taxes for the upper brackets while providing much smaller benefits for the lower income groups. He made Prohibition a constant target.

If the Progressives succeeded in blocking the administration on one measure or another, the administration had little difficulty in preventing adoption of most of the reforms advocated by La Guardia and his fellow insurgents. Most of the Congress during the Harding-Coolidge years believed that no ill could befall the country and that prosperity would be insured, if the Government encouraged large-scale business enterprise by special privileges, discouraged the organization of labor unions, strengthened the Prohibition laws, and followed a policy of isolationism in foreign affairs. Press, pulpit, classroom, movie screen, and all public platforms popularized this view. Those who differed ran the chance of being called "Bolsheviks." The awakening was still to come.

Gemma La Guardia arrived early in the summer of 1924 to visit her brother. The visit was pleasant, but Fiorello did not permit her presence in New York to divert him from building the personal organization he needed to ensure his re-election.

The La Guardia headquarters were on the ground floor of an old brownstone on East 116th Street. It was furnished with a few splintery desks, some old typewriters, a mimeograph machine, and rows of wooden folding chairs. Gemma was not impressed with the place, but to La Guardia's constituents it was a refuge and a stronghold. For anyone in the Twentieth District who had a problem, the word was, "Go see La Guardia. He will help you." Whether it was a wayward youth in trouble, a complaint against a landlord, the complications of acquiring citizenship, hospital care, or food for a needy family—there was always aid and comfort at the La Guardia club.

At regular intervals, the Major sent the voters written reports of his activities and opinions. They always began: "My dear Constituents— In keeping with my ideas of the duties of a Representative, I desire to submit my report . . ."

They were more than reports. They were also manifestoes, proclamations, pronouncements of principle, and battle-cries.

On June 15, the Congressman made his annual report to a mass meeting at the Star Casino on East 107th Street. It was a large but homey gathering. There were serious-looking young men in shirtsleeves and weatherbeaten graybeards who didn't understand La Guardia's words but who were fiercely aware that he wanted to help. There were mothers carrying babies who occasionally punctuated Fiorello's statements with cries, crows, or gurgles. Gemma had a seat in the front row.

"One reason why I cannot support the Republican platform," Fiorello shouted, "is its vicious immigration law based on prejudice and racial hatred." He had other, equally urgent reasons. The administration of President Harding, who had died a year earlier, was being disgraced from day to day by snowballing revelations of the most massive and shameful corruption in the nation's history. Secretary of the Navy Edwin N. Denby, Secretary of the Interior Albert B. Fall, Attorney General Harry M. Daugherty, and Colonel Charles R. Forbes, Director of the Veterans Bureau, all had resigned in the face of accusations that they had betrayed the public trust. Fall and Forbes eventually were sent to prison. Daugherty escaped by a hair's breadth.

La Guardia summed up his mounting antagonism toward Republicanism as practiced by the Harding-Coolidge regime:

"Some people think they are 'regular' when they are only dumb! As to my choice between loyalty to my party and loyalty to my country, I am for loyalty to my country first. . . . Some people say I am as bad as La Follette. I only wish I were as good as La Follette. . . . What is party regularity? It is never urged (on anyone) until a party asks an individual to do something which he believes is wrong.

"I would rather be right than regular!"

A day or two after the mass meeting, Fiorello had a talk with Louis Espresso. "If I don't get the Republican nomination," said La Guardia, "I'll run as a Progressive and I'll take all the Socialist endorsement I can get."

Louis exploded with anger. "If you bolt from the Party," he said, "you'll bolt without me. You could still run as a Republican, but what you want to do is plain suicide. You've done foolish things before, F.H., and I've always stuck with you, but if you do this, you and I are finished. You just don't know the meaning of loyalty."

Fiorello seized on the word. "Loyalty? To what? Did the machine ever show me any loyalty? They practically apologized to Tammany every time I won an election! I've always fought my own battles. I'm in debt to nobody, Louis!"

But if there was one man to whom "F.H." was in debt, it was Louis Espresso, the straight organization man who had guided him through the basic training of practical politics. Whatever doubts La Guardia may have had, he put quickly and firmly behind him. It was June and nomination time. But no one nominated him. In the second week of August, he allowed the newspapers to announce his candidacy as a Progressive. In the Twentieth Congressional District, the Socialist Party gave up trying to defeat La Guardia and joined him by putting his name on their ballot. The Congressman was no more afraid of being stigmatized by his temporary Socialist label than he was by having had Tammany endorsement to defeat the Socialist, Scott Nearing, in 1918.

Marie Fischer ran the campaign headquarters. After eight years and four election campaigns at La Guardia's side, she had become a seasoned veteran of practical politics in her own right.

Lower Harlem had seldom witnessed such ringing of doorbells, stuffing of mail slots with campaign literature, and outdoor oratory.

What was new in this campaign was the emergence of a younger generation of citizens of immigrant parentage. They felt strongly that, by virtue of their American birth and education, this country belonged to them every bit as much as it did to the Ku Klux Klan and the spokesmen of "Nordic supremacy" in the halls of Congress. This second generation applauded the most furiously when La Guardia said at his Star Casino meeting in June:

"This country is made up of immigrants and as long as these foreigners remained in miserable tenements and ghettos there was no objection against them. But now that they have learned to live up to the American standard of decent apartments and to ask for a living wage, we find opposition to these aliens."

One of the young tenement dwellers who was stirred by La Guardia's militant championship of democracy was twenty-two-year-old, dark-eyed, slope-shouldered Vito Marcantonio.

Marcantonio had met La Guardia three years earlier at an assembly program in De Witt Clinton High School which the Aldermanic President was attending as a guest. Vito, a senior student, made a speech which aroused the interest of the distinguished visitor. In it he advocated a Federal system of old-age pensions and unemployment insurance. In his own address to the students, La Guardia took up young Vito's theme.

They met again during the 1924 campaign. Vito was going to New York University Law School. A fiery, implacable fighter, he became a courageous leader of a political commando group. For the group, no hours were too early or too late, no task too difficult, to spread the message in English, Italian, and Yiddish: "Vote for Fiorello H. La Guardia." The youths "Marc" had assembled were ready not only to distribute handbills but to do bare-knuckles battle with Tammany strong-arm squads who wanted to disrupt campaign meetings or keep La Guardia watchers out of polling places.

The bond which developed between La Guardia and Marcantonio became lifelong. Except for one troubled year, they enjoyed the mutual respect and affection that might exist between a distinguished father and a talented son. The tie could hardly have been stronger if Vito had really been his son.

The young people injected a new exuberance into the campaign. Two of them wrote a campaign song:

Fiorello H. La Guardia,
We're with you,
And we'll be with you to the end!
Fiorello H. La Guardia,
Harlem needs a man like you in Congress:
You voted for the Soldiers' Bonus,
Helped the Immigrants,
And fought in Congress for us!
Fiorello H. La Guardia,
With a record like yours Harlem needs you.

The song did good service in the campaign, but one of the abiding mysteries of American politics is how its words were ever sung to the tune of "On the Road to Mandalay."

Fiorello won the election by a substantial majority, defeating the Democrat, Henry Frank, whom he had beaten in 1922 and the Republican, Isaac Siegel, whom he had helped to elect in 1918.

Gemma sailed back to the old country just about the time the campaign ended. Fiorello's victory was the occasion for a telegram of congratulations from his brother Richard, who was then acting principal of the printing school at the New Jersey State Prison. The coolness that had sprung up between them a few years earlier because Fiorello had refused to use political influence to help him get a job was poignantly evident in his message:

"Dear brother: Mary and the children join me in extending to you our most sincere congratulations on your victorious result. While none of us are personally in favor of the party which you are now a member of, we realize, however, the special handicap you had in succeeding as well as you did."

Fiorello had little in common with Gemma or Richard. Dearer to his heart were the patient, strong-minded Marie Fischer and this new warrior of East Harlem, Vito Marcantonio. There are times when the blood tie is a lesser bond than the comradeship of battle.

CHAPTER 13

A Spade Is a Spade

During a House committee meeting one afternoon in 1925, La Guardia of New York listened impatiently to Representative Blanton of Texas talk about a bill of minor importance. As Blanton droned on, La Guardia's irritation mounted steadily. "Let me say to the gentleman from Texas," he interjected, "that he is not the sole brains of the District of Columbia Committee."

Blanton retorted, "The gentleman from New York is not expected to agree to any bill the Democrats or the Republicans bring in."

"Does the gentleman from Texas agree to the bill?" demanded the scrappy little New Yorker.

Blanton ignored him. "When I first came here, he was an orthodox Republican. They elected him, he sat with them and organized with them . . . but the Republican Party did not suit him and he began to sit across the aisle occasionally. And the great Democratic Party did not suit him, so he got off in a little corner of New York, where you can find any kind of people, and organized a party of his own."

The clash was unimportant in itself, but it revealed the deep differences between Fiorello H. La Guardia and most of his Congressional colleagues during the ten years he spent in the House from 1923 to 1932. Blanton's comment on La Guardia's career was a simple statement of fact which he intended as an indictment. In many quarters, it was regarded as such.

Wasn't it reprehensible for a man to buck "the party line"? And wasn't it even worse to switch from one party to the other? Why would a man who might be a solid Republican officeholder all his life want to be elected by "any kind of people" on the Socialist ticket? And such people! Aliens, who adored him because he spoke their languages and fought their petty battles for lower rent and cheaper meat. Couldn't the man ever see the big picture? Didn't he understand that the only way to keep American prosperity going ever onward and upward was to give large-scale business enterprise a free hand?

Such criticisms were of small concern to the man from East Harlem. The affection, close to idolatry, which the Little Flower received from his followers in Manhattan, more than made up for Blanton's slur.

When Fiorello was elected New York State Grand Master of the Sons of Italy that year, two brawny women delegates hoisted him to their shoulders and paraded him around the hall as hundreds cheered. The demonstration expressed more than personal admiration. It was the climax of a two-year struggle between the pro- and anti-Mussolini factions within the organization. La Guardia's election was a triumph for the democratic-minded Italian-Americans over Il Duce's Fascist supporters.

The Little Flower tried to keep close to the people he represented. If they did not come to him, he went to them. He tried, consistently, to reveal the mysteries of government as practiced on Capitol Hill. He wanted the voters to be aware of their importance. Periodically, he reported to them from the rostrum of overflowing meeting halls and sent them printed accounts of his Congressional activities.

In Washington, he kept up a steady barrage against the legislative hairsplitters who always had solid excuses for refusing to act in the interests of the common people and never failed to come up with broad and noble reasons for aiding the rich. It was unbelievable to La Guardia, for instance, that any American could want to operate an industry which derived its profits from the low-wage labor of children. "Leaving sick bed. Express purpose vote for child-labor amendment," he wired to a trade union organization on April 16, 1924. At stake was a Constitutional amendment which was adopted by Congress but never ratified by the necessary number of states.

The little man in the big black hat did not stop arguing against the Johnson-Reed Act, which raised barriers against immigration from southern and eastern Europe, after its passage in 1924. When dispossessed nobility or reigning royalty, such as the Russian Grand Duke Boris or Queen Marie of Roumania, docked at New York, the Great Commoner of East Harlem wrote peppery letters to the Department of Labor, which administered the immigration laws. He demanded to know "whether these repudiated, unemployed, shiftless dukes and grand dukes" were likely to become public charges. The spectacle of Americans kowtowing to visiting nobility disgusted him. He condemned it as being un-American, shocking, ridiculously stupid.

He heaped scorn on a bill which proposed to establish a public shooting ground near a migratory bird refuge:

"I am for conservation of bird life; but when I want advice on the subject, I refuse to take it from a paid agent of ammunition and gun makers! If this bill is to pass, gentlemen, let there be no hypocrisy about it. Let it be known as 'The Bird Slaughter Bill.' "

That was only a sideswipe, in passing, at a routine lobbyist trick for deceiving the public. La Guardia just couldn't bear to hear a spade called anything but a spade. On the issue of living costs, he fought a Ten Years' War. When retail meat prices rose alarmingly in the winter of 1925-26, Fiorello turned himself into a one-man investigating committee. He learned that the price of cattle had not risen at the Chicago stockyards, but that New York butchers were charging more because they had to pay higher prices to the meat packers. When he asked the Department of Agriculture to conduct an official investigation, Secretary William Jardine replied that it couldn't be done. La Guardia rose from his seat in the House to roast the administration and the meat packers to a turn:

"The Department of Agriculture wanted to aid in our fight

against the high prices of meat," he said, "and they sent me this pamphlet, 'Lamb and Mutton, and Their Uses in the Diet.'

"Never mind the diet, say we to the Department. We know all about lamb but, as I told you the other day, ninety per cent of the people of New York City cannot *afford* to eat lamb chops. Why, I have right here with me now——" he paused to grope around in his pockets, "where is it? Oh, yes, here it is in my vest pocket, thirty cents worth of lamb." And he held up a forlorn looking sliver of meat and bone. Both the floor and the visitors' gallery broke into laughter and there were especially appreciative chuckles from the press gallery.

"I believe it is high time that this matter of price-fixing be stopped, and a better system of distribution be created," he continued. "Unless something is done, I will say that the people of New York will stop eating meat. It will be no difficulty at all to arrange a city-wide meat strike in twenty-four hours . . . We want to stop this exploitation. We want to restore the American breakfast to the children of this age." This threat of a consumers' strike and protests by community organizations succeeded in bringing some price relief.

Occasionally he won a clear-cut victory. In 1926, La Guardia in the House and Robert M. La Follette, Jr., in the Senate, introduced resolutions to investigate the Ward Food Products Corporation, which controlled the huge Ward, Continental, and General baking companies. Three days later, the Department of Justice started a court action charging William B. Ward and other businessmen with violating the antitrust laws. To make sure the issue wasn't forgotten, Fiorello had consumer organizations and prominent social workers hold a mass meeting in New York's Carnegie Hall. The theme of the meeting was that the existence of the enormous Ward combination would force small bakers out of business and boost retail bread prices because competition would be eliminated. On April 3, 1926, the Government won its suit to break up the Ward monopoly.

He launched a rebellion which helped defeat the administration's bill to sell the Muscle Shoals hydroelectric plant on the Tennessee River to Henry Ford. Rescued from private ownership, this became, in 1933, the basis of the huge regional development administered by the Tennessee Valley Authority (TVA), a Government-owned corporation. As a junior ally of Senator Norris, La Guardia fought all through the twenties for such a corporation. The Joint Resolution which he and the Senator introduced in 1928 was passed by Congress, only to be vetoed by President Coolidge. A similar bill, passed in 1931, was vetoed by President Hoover. But La Guardia's impassioned speeches on behalf of publicly owned power plants reveal him as an early New Dealer.

He continued the fights he had begun in his first term against Prohibition, rent gouging, unfair taxation, and harsh applications of the new immigration laws.

During this Washington decade, he combined the energies of a crusader, the conscience of a social critic, the instincts of a master propagandist, and the knowledge of an expert on almost every issue under discussion. If he could accomplish little else, he could challenge political and legislative pretenses. He could be the little boy who cried out to all the people that the emperor wore no clothes. Men like Blanton sometimes triggered him into rough speech or into clowning outrageously. His antics were not always spontaneous. Behind his stormy behavior there was a shrewd knack for keeping himself in the headlines.

He could be dignified and formal, but he was never stuffy. He could be angry almost to the point of violence, but he was never grim. His hair-trigger temper was balanced by lively wit and the gift of laughter.

With an adroit thrust he once silenced his opponent, Henry Frank, who solicited Jewish votes because he was himself Jewish. "After all, La Guardia asked, "is he looking for a job as a *schamas* (custodian of a synagogue) or does he want to be elected Congressman?"

Blanton once said on the floor of the House that any Congressman who violated the Prohibition law ought to be removed from office. Fiorello interrupted, "Then we wouldn't have a quorum here."

During debate on an appropriations bill, Wingo of Arkansas, who was reputedly vain about his appearance, engaged the rumpled little New Yorker in an exchange of discourtesies. Criti-

cizing an expenditure for the adornment of a Federal building in
New York City, Wingo asked: "Does the gentleman from New
York know what a façade is?"

La Guardia replied, "Of course. Does the gentleman from
Arkansas?"

"Yes, it is the same thing to a building that a snout is to a hog.
It is the front part of it."

La Guardia's retort was memorable: "If the gentleman from
Arkansas was less interested in his façade and more in the inside
of his head, he'd be a better legislator."

In the summer of 1926, New York City was having troubles
of its own, as usual. Some forty thousand members of the International Ladies Garment Workers Union were on strike. In
Mayor James J. Walker's town, large strikes were not genteel occasions. The Police Department looked the other way when
detachments of ruffians hired by employers terrorized the
strikers. Murder was not always excluded from the program.
Police officials were lightning quick to respond, however, to employers' complaints against picketing.

One sultry morning in July, some twenty thousand men and
women lined up in the side streets of the garment district waiting for the signal to form a parade along Seventh Avenue. They
intended to assert, in a body, the right of peaceful picketing which the Police Department had systematically denied them.
They stepped into Seventh Avenue at noon, four abreast, standard bearers and musicians leading the way. The parade ended almost as soon as it had begun. Mounted policemen galloped into
the column with nightsticks swinging. Patrolmen on foot herded
marchers into doorways to wait for the patrol wagons and am-
bulances which would haul them away.

It was one of those events which occasionally shocks a community out of its accustomed indifference to labor disputes. In
New York, traditionally known as "a union town," this outburst
of violence was doubly disturbing.

Fiorello was enraged. "We have friend Mayor Walker to
thank for this unnecessary brutality," he roared. "They'll hear
from me." The brutal assault of Mayor Walker's police on Seventh

Avenue was more than a local matter to La Guardia. It was added evidence in support of the belief he shared with Senator Norris and other progressives that new laws were needed to provide fair methods of negotiation in labor-management disputes.

It was a month before Fiorello took any personal action. When he found that the arrest of pickets continued to be a daily occurrence, he informed the press that he was going to join a picket line at the offices of the employers' association. Police, reporters, and photographers were on hand for the occasion. They stood watch as the Congressman plodded along earnestly in the double file of marchers wearing strike placards. At a signal from their sergeant, four policemen herded all the pickets except La Guardia against the wall of the building and told them they were under arrest.

Standing alone on the hot sidewalk, the chubby legislator looked up and cried, "Why don't you arrest me?"

"I don't have any order," the sergeant answered.

"I'm doing exactly what they did," LaGuardia persisted. "I'm picketing!"

The sergeant flushed with anger and embarrassment. "It doesn't make any difference. We're not arresting you. You can go home. The show is over."

It wasn't. The reporters swarmed around and La Guardia drove his point home. If the picketing was illegal, it was just as illegal for him as for the others. The fact that the police didn't arrest him showed they had a choice in the matter. But where the strikers were concerned, the police exercised their choice in favor of the employers.

"Our picketing was absolutely peaceful and lawful," he declared "You saw it. We marched along the sidewalk in a column of two and we were careful not to block traffic. I'll have more to say about this tonight at the protest meeting in Madison Square Garden."

Before the strike was over, it was time for La Guardia's 1926 campaign for re-election. He had been a man without a party since the dwindling of the Progressive movement and the death of the elder La Follette a year earlier. At the invitation of Sam

Koenig, he accepted the Republican nomination, with his fingers crossed, as usual. There was considerable hullabaloo in the newspapers concerning his decision. His statement in 1924, "I'd rather be right than regular," was brought back to haunt him. A *New York Times* editorial headed "FORCED ADOPTION" explained why: "The Republicans need him a good deal more than he needs them." Actually, the need was mutual.

After a hard-fought campaign, he won re-election by the smallest handful of votes in his career. Returning to Washington, he resumed his old crusades and found new ones to which he could lend his Barnumlike talents for political showmanship.

In 1927, when Charles Lindbergh became a national hero by making the first solo flight across the Atlantic, from New York to Paris, Major La Guardia used the favorable moment of mass enthusiasm for "Lindy's" feat to dramatize his own longstanding concern for the development of American aviation. He flew as a passenger over West Point to drop flowers on the graduating exercises of the United States Military Academy because the son of a Washington colleague was among the cadets. A month later, he played "aerial golf" in the sky over the Dunwoodie course at Yonkers, by dropping golf balls to his team below.

He wound up skylarking that summer on a 2,600-mile air jaunt from Staten Island, New York, to Hibbing, Minnesota, and back. The pilot was his wartime friend, Lieutenant Marion L. Elliott. Because their plane traveled slowly and made much noise they dubbed it "The Politician."

La Guardia had been advocating the construction of a municipal airport for New York City, but had made no headway. He saw to it that when "The Politician" was ready to return to its home field, there were plenty of newspapermen on hand to meet him. That was the reason for the flight.

"Cleveland has a splendid municipal airport," said La Guardia. "Chicago already has picked a wonderful location." Then he added, "Here in New York the need for an airport has become most urgent. The railways are blocking the erection of a terminal because they are afraid of the competition of air travel."

It would be almost eleven years before the first shovelful of earth was turned for the creation of New York City's big municipal airport, but Fiorello had a habit of looking a long way ahead. In this instance, it was a habit that has made the phrase "La Guardia Field" a commonplace along the airlanes of the world.

CHAPTER 14

The Twenty-Ninth of October

"IT IS DISGRACEFUL HOW THE LAST SESSION OF CONGRESS simply refused to consider any progressive legislation," La Guardia wrote in 1925 in a report to his constituents.

The Congressional mood was no different after his re-election in 1928. The whole country was prosperity-happy, even though the prosperity was only partly real.

The national income, money earned by individuals or companies in wages, commissions, profits, and other forms, was $89,500,000,000. This was $18,000,000,000 more than in 1925. Total profits for all corporations had jumped from $9,300,000,000 to $12,700,000,000. There was much money in banks that people could borrow if they were considered good risks for repayment. If not, they could buy almost anything they wished on the installment plan. About fifteen per cent of all retail sales, or $6,000,000,-000 worth of goods moved out of the stores that year on a "buy-now-pay-later" basis.

A wage-earner who wanted to take a chance with his rent money could even get rich on the installment plan by "playing the market" (or so people thought). That is, he could engage in stock trading through a broker who represented him and many other clients on the New York Stock Exchange or the Curb Exchange. This dangerous but fascinating game was played as follows:

For $100 in real money, a person could buy a $1000 worth of stock shares "on margin." The broker advanced the other $900 and kept his stock certificates as security. But where did the broker get the $900 to lend? He borrowed it from a bank. The bank charged interest and the broker charged the investor more interest than he paid.

When the prices of the stocks went up high enough to suit him, the client ordered his broker to sell. The client made a profit, which he immediately invested in more stocks.

If the stocks started to go down, the broker asked him to put up a little more money. If the investor couldn't, the broker sold the stocks, took out the $900 owed to him, plus the interest and service charges, and gave the client what was left. And if the sale didn't bring in enough to pay what was owed, the investor made up the difference out of next month's rent money or by borrowing from an uncle.

But in 1928, no one worried. The idea was firmly fixed in the mind of the nation that all "downs" in the stock market were only temporary. Everyone was convinced, except for a few radicals and calamity criers like La Guardia, that there was only one way for stocks to go—up, Up, UP! Everyone would go on making money: the investor, the broker, the banks, and the industries on whose prosperity investors were gambling every time they bought a few shares of General Motors or Amalgamated Baseball Bat. This was the national mood. Hadn't Herbert Hoover said in mid-1928, "We in America are nearer the triumph over poverty than ever before in the history of any land"? Actually, only a small percentage of the population, probably no more than three million shareholders were involved in this great game of Wall Street roulette.

Uncle Sam had shaved off his chin whiskers and was behaving like a Good-Time Charlie. His wife was making vile-tasting "home brew" beer in the kitchen, learning to smoke cigarettes, and practicing the steps of the "Charleston" or the "Black Bottom" while pushing her unpaid-for vacuum cleaner around the parlor. Everyone felt young and everyone was going to be rich, except—the four million unemployed, the six and a half million who were living on incomes of less than three thousand dollars a year, the several million farmers whose places were mort-gaged to the tip of the old cow's tail, and the millions of factory workers who lived from one pay day to the next. There was pros-perity to be sure, but it rested on a very shaky foundation.

"Whatever may be said about prosperity today," La Guardia admonished his House colleagues, "and I believe that a great deal of that prosperity is simply stock-ticker prosperity, the fact re-mains that there is considerable unemployment."

On other occasions, he lashed out at low wages and long hours for industrial workers. He told a Congressional committee, "It is impossible to enjoy the blessings of liberty on an empty stomach."

He supported a measure to establish an adequate minimum wage in some industries. Though the bill did not go through, the Major predicted that eventually there would have to be a broad Federal minimum wage law.

In March, 1928, he introduced a bill for a seventy-five-mil-lion-dollar fund for the welfare of children in needy families. It was quickly buried by its opponents.

While newspapers in most of the country were printing editorials praising the nation's financial and industrial leaders as the architects of a fabulous American prosperity, Fiorello was taking an opposite view. In his own newspaper column in the *New York Graphic*, for which he had been writing since 1925 as "America's Most Liberal Congressman," he said:

"Mr. Andrew Mellon (Secretary of the Treasury and then reputed to be one of the three richest men in the United States) is invariably described as one of the financial giants of the world . . . It is true that Messrs. Mellon, Ford, Rockefeller, Schwab, Morgan, and a great many others increased their for-tunes every year.

"The writer will not dispute the financial genius of any of these gentlemen. But can any of them improve on the financial genius of Mrs. Mary Esposito, or Mrs. Rebecca Epstein, or Mrs. Maggie Flynn, who keep house in a city tenement, raise six chil-dren on a weekly envelope containing thirty dollars, try to send their children to school warmly and properly clad, pay ex-orbitant gas and electric bills, and endeavor to provide meat at

least once a day for the family? That's financial genius of the
highest order . . . Let some of our greatest financial geniuses try
housekeeping in a New York tenement under these conditions
and get a real test of their financial wizardry! How about trying to make the lot of the American family better as a real test of
public service—rather than the individual accumulation of personal fortunes? "

Despite the presence of a few surviving Progressives (they
often differed with him on such issues as Prohibition, immigration, or farm relief), La Guardia began to feel increasingly
alone in Washington. His one sure ally was Marie Fischer who
ran his office and, as much as she dared, his life. She was his secretary, research assistant, press attaché, and protector. In the years
since 1922, she had become a sort of Assistant Congresswoman
from the Twentieth District.

After fifteen years of association with Marie, and after seven
years as a widower, it occurred to Major La Guardia that it might
be a good idea to marry this devoted and invaluable woman. She
thought it was a good idea, too. She had thought so for years.
They were married in Washington on February 28, 1929, by
Representative Ole J. Kvale of Minnesota, an ordained minister
of Marie's Lutheran persuasion, who was a personal friend and
fellow roomer of Fiorello in the capital. After a wedding breakfast, the couple headed for their desks in the House Office Building. There was work to do.

A good deal of their work that year was connected with the
growing likelihood that Fiorello could corral the nomination to
oppose James J. Walker's bid for re-election as Mayor of New
York that fall. He had been waiting patiently for the Republicans
to make good their promise of 1919 which was broken in 1921.
At last, he was to have his big chance to twist the Tammany
Tiger's tail.

There were obstacles, of course. The more conservative
upper-class Republican leaders wanted to nominate Congresswoman Ruth Pratt, a sure loser, from the Upper East Side "silk
stocking" district. Fiorello handled that by threatening that he
would refuse to support any of the Republican candidates. He
would sit out the whole campaign in Bermuda. The following

year, he warned, he would oppose the Republican candidate for governor. With Franklin D. Roosevelt, the anti-Tammany Democrat, occupying the Governor's mansion in Albany, he could have done so without losing face.

As usual, La Guardia was a thorn in the side of the Republican leadership. But they had to put up with that vote-getter. They had to give him the nomination.

On August 1, 1929, from the stage of Manhattan's Mecca Temple, Fiorello surveyed the mechanical smiles and heard the less than rafter-shaking cheers with which the fifteen hundred assembled party workers greeted his nomination. His own answering smile was not entirely heartfelt. Most of them either didn't want him to win or didn't think he could. No matter. He lost no time in reminding them that La Guardia was a man who plays for keeps.

"I accept the nomination," he said. "Your remarks generally are most flattering. I appreciate the many nice things you have said about me. Thanks. Now let's get down to business . . ."

La Guardia went into the campaign hopefully. He felt sure of solid support from the labor unions, veterans organizations, Italian-American voters groups, and housewives in wage-earning families who were concerned with the cost of living. Negro groups remembered his defense that April of Representative Oscar De Priest against Southern Congressmen who had objected to having De Priest as a neighbor in the House Office Building. La Guardia had sent Speaker Nicholas Longworth a telegram saying he would be glad to have "our colleague, the gentleman from Illinois, Mr. De Priest, next to my office . . ." De Priest thanked the Major but added, "Those who do not like to be near me can move. I have no objection to any member making a fool of himself."

La Guardia had lined up the backing of such Ivy League Republicans as Keyes Winter, who became his campaign manager; Alderman Joseph Clark Baldwin III, a vice-president of the Murray Hill Trust Company; Ogden L. Mills; and a handful of other bankers and lawyers of spotless respectability and enviable social standing. His public endorsers, whatever they may have thought of him privately, included Colonel Theodore Roosevelt,

Jr., Secretary of State Henry L. Stimson, R.C.A. President James
G. Harboard, Columbia University President Nicholas Murray
Butler.

Nevertheless, he was facing formidable opposition from the
Socialists, whose candidate was Norman Thomas, from the Old
Guard Republicans, who refused to contribute to his campaign
fund, and from Jimmy Walker's powerful Tammany machine.

"Gentleman Jimmy" was no tailor's dummy, as a La Guardia
enthusiast had implied. He could make some of the same claims
as Fiorello. He was a "man of the people" born of immigrant parents; he was against Prohibition; and, to uncritical New Yorkers,
he had made a good record as a member of the State Legislature.
His ready wit and his great capacity for making friends with one
man, or with five thousand, marked him as the most magnetic
Tammany personality who ever emptied the city's treasury.

Fiorello attacked the Walker regime unmercifully. There
was hardly a Tammany politician, he charged, who would care
to tell where all the money in his bank account really came from.
Somehow, a promissory note had fallen into La Guardia's hands
showing that Magistrate Albert H. Vitale, a loyal Tammany man,
had received $19,940 from Arnold Rothstein, an important
gambler who had been murdered at the Park Central Hotel in
November, 1928. Fiorello made the most of the situation.

He repeated and elaborated ex-Mayor Hylan's charges that
"The present administration is the most wasteful and extravagant
in the history of New York and the slimy trail of waste, reckless-
ness, and corruption is unparalleled since the days of Boss
Tweed," and that "While the city treasury is being looted of millions, the Mayor was dawdling away his time . . . in Holly-
wood and on Broadway."

To an endless barrage of such charges, Walker replied
with wisecracking loftiness that while he was willing to go as far
as the gutter to defend himself, he refused to go down into the
sewer. In that last year of those happy-go-lucky 1920's, he didn't
need to. Many voters were more interested in hearing ex-song-
writer Jimmy Walker sing his hit number, "Will You Love Me in
December as You Do in May," than in his answers to La
Guardia's accusations. People tolerated good-natured, entertain-

ing larceny. New Yorkers who went out of their way to shop at Macy's because everything was "six per cent less" there, didn't seem to mind if Jimmy's administration caused their taxes to be ten per cent more. They shopped at Macy's because "it's smart to be thrifty," but, in Jimmy Walker's case, they were quite ready to believe that "it's smart to be shifty."

The rumpled little Republican wouldn't let up. At a meeting of the Irish-American League, which liked Fiorello because he was a longtime supporter of Irish independence, he struck a prize fighting posture and cried:

"I've got Jimmy in a corner! He can't move! He's groggy! This is a real fight. Come out and fight like a man, Jimmy."

The following night, October 28, he spoke in a more dignified but equally fiery mood to a trade union rally, declaring:

"I pledge my word that the Eight-Hour Law and all other legislation placed on the statute books, after ages of discrimination against the toiler, shall be enforced to the limit of my ability. After my election, I will not permit my Police Commissioner to turn the police force of this great city into a private, strike-breaking, union-busting agency."

It was no use. The magic of prosperity, Tammany strength, Republican disunity, and mass indifference proved too tough a combination to beat. At the Hotel Cadillac campaign headquarters run by Marie La Guardia, there was ceaseless activity. Wherever he could, young Vito Marcantonio worked wonders of campaigning with his band of devoted young La Guardians who called themselves Gibboni, an Italian word of uncertain East Harlem coinage. In vain did they sing at campaign rallies, to the tune of the Marine's Hymn, the words written by Grace Murphy:

> Down to City Hall we're marching
> For La Guardia's bound for there,
> With his banners waving victory
> To give Tammany the air.
> We have watched the circus long enough;
> Let the Tiger scratch and bawl.
> We are following La Guardia
> To the doors of City Hall.

> Seven times he's won elections,
> Seven times he's reached the top.
> He is proud he's an American
> And he's proud he is a wop!
> Just remember Chris Columbus . . .
> Now join in the chorus all . . .
> We are following La Guardia
> To his chair in City Hall.

Defeat was inevitable, but it was made even more certain by an event which reduced the election campaign to a position of secondary importance. On Tuesday, October 29, a week before Election Day, the stock prices which everyone thought could go only upward, took the most sickening downward plunge in the 117-year history of Wall Street. During the regular five-hour trading day on the New York Stock Exchange, 16,400,000 shares were sold at ruinous prices. It was not the first such day that year, nor the last, but it was the worst.

Large and small shareholders in the stocks of the nation's industries—steel, coal, automobiles, chemicals, oil, electric power —became penniless overnight. They saw their savings and their dreams of a comfortable future vanish. What was worse, they found themselves confronted by debts they could not repay with the easy money they hoped to make tomorrow or next week. What hope was left when a stock such as General Electric dropped from a high price of $403 a share earlier in the year to $210 on October 29, with hundreds of other stocks following suit? It was no longer summertime and the living was no longer easy.

The preoccupied New Yorkers who went to the polls on Tuesday, November 5, gave Jimmy Walker 865,000 votes. La Guardia was unable to muster more than 368,000. Even the 175,000 votes he might have picked up from Norman Thomas, if the Socialists had supported no candidate of their own, would have been of no help.

After sending a telegram to Walker conceding the election and congratulating him, Fiorello emerged from his office at the Cadillac Hotel to face his supporters and well-wishers. His cheeks were tear-stained, his words were few: "I thank you all, and re-member, when you go out of here, smile!"

Someone cried out, "He is our fighting Congressman still!" and it was Fiorello's turn to smile, somewhat grimly. He had a number of important questions to raise with President Hoover's administration. What had become of the glib talk about "a chicken in every pot and two cars in every garage?" And what about the boast that poverty could be abolished merely by continuing the Coolidge-Hoover policies of permissiveness and tender loving care for Big Business?

During most of 1929, there had been an increasing number of letters to La Guardia from men who wanted help in finding jobs. Most of the letters were from people he had never met, people who lived outside his district and had non-Italian, non-immigrant names. All these appeals had a tone of urgency and distress he had not encountered in earlier letters from the public. Most of them sounded like the one from Luke Johnson, a carpenter: "For God's sake," he wrote, "please help me out as I need work in the worst way or I will be put out on the street as my rent is due."

In Fiorello's book, there was a reckoning due in Washington, too.

CHAPTER 15

The Great Depression

WHAT HAD GONE WRONG? WHAT WAS THE REAL MEANing of the Wall Street crash? Were things going to get better or worse?

That's what everyone was asking when La Guardia went back to Washington in December, 1929.

The Hoover administration asserted there was nothing seriously wrong. On October 25, a day after the big stock market crash which preceded the shattering "Black Tuesday" of October 29, the President had said, "The fundamental business of the country is on a sound and prosperous basis."

Hoover's wildly optimistic view was supported by the nation's most respected leaders of finance and industry. John D. Rockefeller said, "Believing that fundamental conditions of the country are sound . . . my son and I have for some days been purchasing sound common stocks."

Even two months later, in January, 1930, Secretary of the Treasury Mellon announced, "I can see nothing . . . in the present situation that is either menacing or warrants pessimism."

In the years that followed, the phrase "business is fundamentally sound" became an ironic taunt of millions of embittered Americans.

During and after World War I, the prices of stocks rose steadily because American industry grew like Jack's beanstalk.

More factories produced more goods, in less time, than ever before. And the goods were sold in greater quantities than ever, at home and overseas.

The profits of the big industrial corporations and banking institutions rolled in so fast that they had to be reinvested quickly and lavishly to keep the nation's bank vaults from overflowing with idle money. Investment in the stocks of the industries that produced such fabulous profits seemed to be a smart move. It was considered an even smarter move to form new companies which could make money simply by selling their stocks.

Just the same, this could not go on forever. Neither the people of the United States nor those of other countries could buy everything that American industry produced. Earnings had risen thirteen per cent between 1921 and 1928, but this increased buying power was not enough. To keep business going, it was necessary to encourage installment buying at home and to lend foreign nations huge sums with which to buy American products. The time came when there was no way to keep selling the vast output of our industries, at home or abroad, for cash or for credit.

The October, 1929, stock market crash was nothing but a terrified premonition of the business world that the Coolidge-Hoover New Era of instant profit was on its way out. Factories and mines began to cut back production or to close down entirely. As work stopped, wages stopped. There were more and more people who could buy less and less. This caused other industries to slow down. Farmers had to sell their products for less. Thus, they had less money to spend, which caused further unemployment in industry. If ever there was a vicious circle, this was it.

The leaders of government, business, and public opinion remained reluctant to face the fact that the nation was on the verge of economic disaster. The words "panic" and "crisis" were avoided but a more genteel term began to be heard in the land— *depression*.

What was this tragic episode in our history? How can the well-fed and exuberant generations that have followed the event

Plate 1. The Music Club, 1896. (G) Gemma, (R) Richard, (F) Fiorello (cornetist); Achille La Guardia.

Plate 2. Awaiting arrival of Coxey's Army; the Capitol, Washington, 1894.

Plate 3. Bride and groom: Thea and Fiorello; left, Louis
Espresso. March, 1919.

Plate 4. On trip to West Coast in 1932, La Guardia seeks out his Prescott, Arizona, schoolteacher, Mrs. Lynna Stockton.

Plate 5. Apple vending, a short-lived substitute for jobs. Washington, 1930.

Plate 6. Bonus Marchers fighting eviction from shelter. Washington, July 1932.

Plate 7. Contingent of jobless college alumni assemble at Columbia University for trip to Washington to protest plight of professionals. New York, 1933.

Plate 8. Rent-free Hoovervilles, Central Park Lower Reservoir. New York, 1933.

Plate 9. Leader addressing Hunger Marchers. Columbus, Ohio, 1935.

Plate 10. Unemployed line up in Times Square for food. New York, 1933.

Plate 11. Mayor and Senator Robert F. Wagner, Sr., at cornerstone laying of Williamsburg Public Housing Project. Brooklyn, 1936.

Plate 12. Congressman Vito Marcantonio interviewed by the press after leading demonstration of 10,000 unemployed through city streets. New York, 1936.

Plate 13. Bill Robinson, Jimmy Durante, and the Mayor sample a meal at Municipal Lodging House. New York, 1938.

Plate 14. President Roosevelt, Mayor La Guardia, Mrs. Roosevelt, and Edward J. Flynn, U.S. Commissioner to World's Fair arrive for opening ceremonies April, 1939.

Plate 15. Mayor La Guardia and Mrs. Roosevelt at opening night of *W.P.A.* "Swing Mikado." New York, 1939.

Plate 16. On the job.

Plate 17. Mrs. Roosevelt conferring with the Mayor.

Plate 18. President Roosevelt signing a proclamation designating December 15 as "Bill of Rights Day." La Guardia was the sponsor of the observance.

Plate 19. UNRRA Director General La Guardia tries to comfort a Czech boy in displaced persons camp near Rome. Italy, 1946.

Plate 20. La Guardia packs his personal papers after twelve years at City Hall. December, 1945.

Plates 21-26. The Little Flower is seen here in six typical poses—dictating correspondence in his limousine, conducting the New York Philharmonic, reading the comics on the radio to a city without them because of a newspaper strike, accepting appointment as head of U.S. civil defense from President Roosevelt, visiting the scene of a fire, and relaxing at home with his family.

be made to understand the poverty and mass desperation of the 1930's?

The depression was a drop of $74,000,000,000 in the total value of all the stocks listed on the New York Stock Exchange, in less than three years; five thousand bank failures in which millions of depositors lost more than $3,000,000,000 of their hard-earned cash.

The depression was a factory worker finding a curt dismissal slip in his pay envelope and it was

4,000,000 unemployed in 1929
6,000,000 unemployed in 1930
8,000,000 unemployed in 1931
13,000,000 unemployed in 1932

and estimates running as high as 17,000,000 in 1933. Even in 1938, some eight and a half years after the Wall Street crash, there were 9,000,000 people without jobs.

The depression was a farmer getting a dime a bushel for oats which had cost him thirteen cents to raise. It was the same farmer reading a notice of the foreclosure sale tacked up on his barn door and a million farms passing from the hands of their debt-ridden owners to the banks, insurance companies, and other mortgage-holders.

In the first six months of 1930, in New York City alone, it was 72,800 eviction orders issued by the courts. It was thousands of homeless men and hundreds of homeless women sleeping in Chicago's parks and thousands of families living in makeshift huts built of any flimsy materials they could scavenge, beg, or steal; colonies of the dispossessed, which were quickly given the name "Hoovervilles."

It was the aimless migration of young and old, by the hundreds of thousands—teenagers on freight trains and families in worn-out autos, wandering across the face of the land, searching for food, shelter, jobs—finding just enough to keep them on the cold trail of a half-dead hope that somehow, somewhere, they would find freedom from want.

The depression was a neighborhood grocer saying, "I can't

give you any more credit until you pay me something on what you owe," and millions of people standing in front of welfare agencies for packages of food and clothing, for help in keeping a roof over their heads, for medical aid.

It was children and adults suffering from diseases of semi-starvation, while ranchers slaughtered their flocks of sheep because they could neither sell them nor feed them.

The depression was a sense of worthlessness corroding the self-esteem of able-bodied men who stared at the No Help Wanted signs on padlocked factory gates.

It was headlines saying FATHER OF FIVE DROWNS SELF.

It was a skulking, shuffling big parade of ex-wage earners who had become adept in the arts and crafts of destitution—begging, peddling, shining shoes, killing time, sneaking on and off streetcars without paying the fare, eating in breadlines, sleeping in municipal shelters, keeping warm in public libraries.

It was a bitter joke about a footsore job hunter on a park bench saying to a bird which had besmirched his hat: "For the *rich* you *sing!*"

It was the poor, and the whole country, singing an ironic lament:

> Once I built a railroad,
> Made it run.
> Made it to race against time.
> Once I built a railroad,
> Now it's done.
> Brother, can you spare a dime?
>
> Once I built a tower to the sun,
> Brick and rivet and lime.
> Once I built a tower,
> Now it's done.
> Brother, can you spare a dime? *

The Great Depression was a proud people stunned by the fact that all this could happen so quickly and last so long in the

* Copyright 1932 by Harms, Inc. Copyright renewed. Used by permission.

richest country in the world. The causes of this catastrophe are still being debated.

The national crisis propelled La Guardia into a new kind of national prominence. Always close to his constituents, he understood better than most legislators what was happening not only in his own district but throughout the land. Hungry people were scavenging in garbage cans while tons of food rotted in the fields. Warehouses and stores were filled with clothing while millions of Americans went ragged. There were thousands of empty apartments and houses but men, women, and children had no homes they could call their own.

Jobless men were encouraged to sell apples, as though that would give them a living. Sad-faced, they shivered on street corners beside open crates from which other jobless men might be hungry enough to buy. During the second winter of the crisis, in New York alone, more than five thousand apple peddlers dejectedly polished their unwanted wares, trying to keep their families from starvation by this acceptable new form of begging.

Unbelievable as the grim events of those years may be to any succeeding generation, it remains equally incredible that the President and most of Congress should have opposed any direct help to the industrial unemployed and the impoverished farmers. Through most of his term in office, ending in March, 1933, President Hoover seemed convinced that the moral fiber of the nation would rot if the unemployed were given a square meal at Federal expense, as a matter of right, instead of begging for handouts from overburdened local relief agencies. He had a deep abhorrence of any kind of social legislation. In a speech during the 1928 election campaign, Hoover had said:

"When the war closed . . . we were challenged with a peacetime choice between the American system of rugged individualism and the European philosophy . . . of paternalism and State Socialism."

Hoover's belief in the infallibility of his economic theories (which were to scourge the nation until another president was ready to face the realities of the times) was based on his own success, a saga of nineteenth-century rugged individualism. Born in 1874, he started his working career as a poor Iowa farm boy. In the twenties, he was known internationally as an engineer, an able organizer, a brilliant administrator of relief in devasted post-war Europe, and as a man of great wealth.

He earnestly believed that the way to deal with cyclical economic crises was to exercise a minimum of government inter-ference and to let industry work out its own recovery. Industry had recovered in the past, and he saw no reason to think the sit-uation was different in the twentieth century. "Economic de-pression," he said early in 1930, "cannot be cured by legislative action or executive pronouncement. Producers and consumers must themselves find the remedy."

Fiorello La Guardia thought otherwise. "We must face the actual situation," he insisted in a New York speech. "There is at present unemployment in every industrial center. . . . Uniform labor laws, unemployment insurance, old-age pensions, a shorter work week, these must all be pressed into reality to save this country from a real crisis. We have . . . excess profits and un-employment. The two are inconsistent."

Together with a small group of Progressives, he poured his energies into a continuing struggle for emergency and long-range legislation to help the cities' unemployed and the impov-erished farmers, to create jobs, to protect savings accounts in case of bank failures—in short, to start the nation's wealth flowing back toward the mass of the people so that the nation's economic life could begin again. He directed a steady fire against the ad-ministration and the President, whose pitiful namesakes, Hoover-villes, were spreading across the land.

Most of the lawmakers only shrugged their shoulders. They shared Hoover's belief in "rugged individualism." "You might as well try to prevent the human race from having a disease as to prevent economic grief of this sort," said Oklahoma's Senator Gore.

To those who had ignored his arguments for an ounce of prevention during most of the decade, Fiorello now pleaded in-dignantly for at least a pound of cure. Demanding that Congress should not adjourn for the 1929 Christmas holiday without pass-ing some emergency legislation to help the jobless, he said:

"Mr. Speaker, I desire to call the attention of the House to the economic conditions confronting the country at this time. If Congress were faced today with an epidemic of a contagious disease, it would immediately take the necessary action to meet the situation." They heard him and shrugged again.

He teamed with New York's Democratic Senator Robert F. Wagner, Sr., in order to try to get depression laws passed. Wagner had introduced three bills calling for the kind of action which both men had advocated in earlier years: a Federal employment agency, an emergency program of public works, the systematic gathering of unemployment statistics, and the long-range planning of construction projects as a preparedness measure against future unemployment. The bills were passed by the Senate but opponents in the House did their best, despite La Guardia, to talk them and maneuver them to death. They were eventually passed in watered-down form but were vetoed by the President.

Mass unemployment, and the resulting competition for existing jobs, confronted employers with a powerful temptation to cut wages. There was no Federal minimum wage law. Hoping to prevent wholesale slashing of pay envelopes, La Guardia introduced a House resolution urging that the President call a conference of governors to agree on the passage of uniform labor laws in all forty-eight states. Hoover regarded the plan as needless. He preferred to rely on the unofficial word of the top industrialists that they would not reduce wages in their plants. But Fiorello wanted more than gentlemanly promises. In a speech on July 1, 1930, he warned that:

"There is a school of thought which believes that unemployment is a condition to be taken advantage of, to drag down wages and to lower labor conditions. This school is based on sordid selfishness and lack of vision."

In the second half of the twentieth century, unemployment insurance has become a humdrum, ordinary matter. Everyone knows what it is—a government fund made up of small payments from employers, for the benefit of workers who have lost their jobs. No shame attaches to the factory hand, who makes ninety dollars a week, or the junior executive, who makes two hundred fifty dollars a week, who benefits from it. It has become

part of the American way of life. It was not so in 1930. Despite
the fact that unemployment insurance had been adopted in much
of Western Europe, it was still opposed in the United States by
powerful business interests, Government leaders, and so-called
experts in the social sciences. It was frequently and loudly condemned by conservative opinion makers as "sheer socialism."

Nevertheless, Fiorello insisted that a new kind of lawmaking
would have to be practiced to meet the problems created by the
Depression. Call them socialist or whatever one chose, without
social welfare laws, the Government would have no way of
stopping the Depression and of helping the country back on its
feet. The horrified outcries of the opposition were of small concern to the little Congressman. The worst they could do was to
sharpen his appetite for action. But there was also the matter of
getting re-elected to Congress in November, 1930.

For the first time, Tammany chose a candidate of Italian origin, Vincent Auletta, to oppose the Major. It was a turbulent,
hard-fought contest. Marcantonio's Gibboni demonstrated that
they had lost none of their campaigning abilities. Marie La
Guardia remained an efficient headquarters boss. And the
"lucky corner" at 116th Street and Lexington Avenue was just as
lucky as ever. Despite the fact that Auletta was backed by Gen-
eroso Pope's influential Italian-language daily, *Il Progresso*, Fiorello was sent back to Congress by a margin of one thousand
votes.

When Congress reconvened in December, La Guardia renewed his fight against the Depression by introducing "a bill to
provide for an employment commission, the creation and maintenance of an unemployment insurance fund, and raising necessary revenue therefor." The House, still fearful of doing anything "socialistic," referred the bill to the Ways and Means Committee where it was left to die. La Guardia was accustomed to being in the minority. But for the majority to block one of his
proposals now was about as effective as putting up a picket fence
to shut out a hurricane.

When he discovered that shipbuilding companies with Government contracts were reducing wages, he intimidated them
into restoring the cuts by threatening to have their contracts can-

celed. He wrote to Secretary of Labor Davis proposing a system of job rotation; he urged Mayor Walker to hire more workers for the construction of the George Washington Bridge over the Hudson River; he protested against a six-hundred-man lay off by the Brooklyn Edison Company, and he bawled out the Secretary of the Navy for permitting military bands to play at public gatherings because they were displacing civilian musicians who needed the jobs.

The zeal of La Guardia's efforts to combat the Depression was so great that he felt cheated when another Congressman, Henry Steagall, beat him to the punch in announcing a plan to protect the savings of small bank depositors. To his staff assistant, Ernest Cuneo, who was helping him on a similar plan, Fiorello complained, "He swiped my idea. Nobody ever thought of it before me."

Cuneo, an exceedingly bright, aggressive young man, told his boss that Government insurance for small bank depositors had been thought of thirty years earlier by Louis D. Brandeis and had been successfully introduced in Massachusetts. Fiorello roared, "Why didn't you say so? You've wasted a good deal of my time, Ernest."

In March, 1931, Fiorello was hospitalized for a short time for treatment of an old hip injury he had suffered in the wartime crash of his Caproni bomber. He was therefore unable to attend the conference of Progressives at which Senator George W. Norris hoped to reorganize the kind of mass political movement which the elder Senator La Follette had led in 1924.

From his hospital bed, he wrote to Norris:

"There is a tendency on the part of leaders in both major parties to continue to legislate on fundamentals laid down in the age of the stage coach, the spinning wheel, and tallow candles. This has resulted in the concentration of a great deal of wealth under the control of a few families, with the large masses of workers entirely at their mercy for their very existence . . . We find ourselves . . . with warehouses full, millions of willing workers out of employment and large numbers dependent upon private charities . . .

"Every day as I lie here in bed I try to think what the last

Congress has accomplished to meet the present economic depression. With the exception of additional appropriations for public improvements, nothing constructive was done . . . The one so-called relief measure gave the opportunity to farmers in drought-stricken areas to borrow, when they are so destitute as to be unable to borrow . . . The mere suggestion of constructive help to the industrial workers was met with howls and groans . . .

"If machinery is displacing workers we must shorten the working day and the working week accordingly. This will give the benefit of machinery to all and not only to those who own machinery. The right of a decent living to every willing worker, a citizen of this Republic, is inherent. The dread of unemployment, with its attendant misery and hardship, must be abolished. Unemployment insurance must be provided. Every industry today takes care of depreciation of its machinery. *They have not yet learned to take care of the people who created and work these machines.*"

Throughout his last years in Congress, La Guardia was horrified by the contrast between the reluctance of the Hoover administration to provide direct relief for the victims of the Depression and its willingness to bail out the big business institutions.

In December, 1931, the Hoover administration introduced a bill to create the Reconstruction Finance Corporation with a fund of $2,000,000,000 for loans to banks, insurance companies, railroads, and industrial organizations. Fiorello opposed it fiercely, but it was approved by Congress in January, 1932. During the first half of 1932, the RFC loaned more than $805,000,000 to business and industry. But of the $300,000,000 set aside by the RFC for direct relief to the nation's needy families, only $30,000,000 had been put to work at the end of the year. Three times that amount, $90,000,000, had been loaned to one institution, the Central Republic Bank and Trust Company of Chicago.

What good was it to save business institutions without saving the people? La Guardia asked. Did banks and industries exist to make life better for the people or was it the other way around? Didn't it matter how the ordinary people lived as long as the big businesses could continue to operate with some hope of profit? Fiorello believed passionately that Government help to business enterprise was not enough. There also had to be direct massive help for the impoverished farmers and industrial workers.

When Senator Wagner and Speaker of the House John N. Garner introduced a bill to provide $3,000,000,000 for direct relief and public building projects to create jobs, Fiorello swung enough Republican votes to assure its passage. It was vetoed by the President. Shortly before the end of the session, La Guardia joined with Senator Costigan in offering a bill to set up a Federal lending institution from which unemployed persons would be able to borrow as much as $500 each. Congress adjourned before the bill could be considered.

But well before adjournment, the roly-poly Representative from East Harlem won three major legislative victories which permitted him to end his Congressional career in a blaze of glory.

President Hoover was committed to the idea of running the Government on a "balanced budget." To accomplish this, the President sent two bills to Congress, the Revenue Act of 1932 and an Economy Bill.

The revenue bill called for the largest peacetime tax increase in history. It proposed to raise more than half of its goal of $1,000,000,000 by a sales tax on manufactured goods. When the Ways and Means Committee reported favorably on the bill, little opposition was expected because the Congressional leaders of both parties had agreed to support it. La Guardia flung himself against the bipartisan steamroller like an exploding 105-millimeter shell and stopped it dead in its tracks. Instead of the expected one or two days of debate on details of the bill, a two weeks' battle ensued.

Sales tax, indeed! What about the $3,500,000,000 Andrew Mellon had given back to big corporations and wealthy individuals during his first eight years as Secretary of the Treasury? Call them refunds, credits, abatements, or whatever—it was nothing but Government confirmation of the old saying that "them as has gits," and it was trying to soak the poor with a sales tax to make up the difference. Fiorello thought it was time to shift some of the burden elsewhere. Was it right, was it just, that people who had hardly enough to eat should have to pay a tax on every necessity they bought? On the floor of the House, in the newspapers, over the radio, and on the telephone to his colleagues, his battle cry became "Soak the Rich."

When the messages of "surrender" came in from Congressmen who had decided to join him in voting against the sales tax, Fiorello smiled and remarked to his young aide, Cuneo, "Their consciences are beginning to catch up with them." The sales tax was defeated and La Guardia was hailed in the nation's newspapers as a legislative hero.

To replace the sales tax, there were written into the Revenue Act higher taxes on big estates, big incomes, stock transfers, bonds, expensive jewelry, pleasure boats, golf clubs, and other material accessories of high living. If country club memberships were overlooked, it was by sheer accident. Many of these new sources of tax money were part of a plan which La Guardia had worked out much earlier.

The Economy Bill, by which Hoover hoped to reduce the budget by $250,000,000, received similar treatment from La Guardia. If he could help it, there would be no cuts in veterans' benefits or Government workers' salaries; and there would be no slashing of appropriations for the Children's Bureau, the Office of Education, and other Government agencies which policed Big Business or stood guard over the public's welfare. There weren't any cuts to speak of by the time he finished. Only $38,000,000 of the President's proposed economies were passed.

His third victory, the passage of the Norris-La Guardia Anti-Injunction Act, was the one he might have chosen as his Congressional monument. Into the writing of this law went a whole lifetime's resentment against all the judicial practices which mocked the American belief in equality before the law.

As a lawyer and as a member of the House Judiciary Committee, he knew how easy it was for the courts to prohibit a strike simply because the employer didn't want one. All the employer needed was to ask a judge for an order—known as an injunction—prohibiting the union from talking to strikebreakers, from picketing, or from merely "interfering with the complainant's business." The latter phrase could mean almost anything, including the publication by the union of newspaper advertisements about the strike.

It was not possible, of course, for a labor union to obtain injunctions which would prohibit an employer from operating dangerous machinery without proper safeguards, from overworking his men, underpaying them, or firing them at the whim of a foreman.

Especially distasteful to fair-minded people was the "yellow dog" contract which workers, especially coal miners, were obliged to sign before they were hired. This was simply an agreement on the part of a worker not to join a union. Sometimes the contract was not even signed by the workers. It was put up on bulletin boards or into the pay envelopes. It served notice that joining a union meant immediate unemployment.

In February, 1928, La Guardia went to western Pennsylvania to have a close look at a bitter and bloody conflict between coal miners and mine owners. To reporters who interviewed him in Pittsburgh, he said, "I have never seen such thorough, deliberate cruelty in my life as there displayed against the unfortunate strikers by the coal operators and their army of Coal and Iron Police." (This was a private force authorized under a Pennsylvania state law which was eventually repealed.) "Imagine, gentlemen, a private army with its private jails where miners are unlawfully detained and assaulted . . . Saturday I shall hear the operators' side of the case, if they will talk to me. But it will take a lot of explaining to account for men walking along the ridge as at Brewster and firing into the barracks of these suffering miners."

What he saw in Pennsylvania made him more determined than ever to outlaw the use of injunctions in labor disputes. The anti-injunction bill was piloted through the Senate by Nebraska's George Norris while La Guardia saw it through the House in March, 1932. Both chambers passed it by overwhelming majorities. It specifically outlawed the "yellow dog" contract, and virtually put an end to the unjust use of antilabor injunctions. In the years that followed, many states passed "Little Norris-La Guardia Acts."

For months after the stock market crash, the American economy lay flat on its back looking up at the circle of trouble experts who hovered over it as they exchanged conflicting advice on how to administer first aid. The futility, the professorial empty-headedness, and the insincerity of much of this advice might have been amusing if the American economy had consisted only of facts and figures. Tragically, it also consisted of people, and it was the people who were getting hurt.

Slowly but inevitably, as life became worse for more people, as jobs grew scarcer, as farmers lost their land in foreclosures, and small businessmen lost their savings in bank failures, bewilderment and desperation grew. Desperation was bound to turn into resentment, and the resentment was bound to express itself in action, when the dispossessed and the hungry realized that unemployment was not their fault.

In New York, as early as March 6, 1930, there was a demonstration of some 75,000, organized by the Communist-led Unemployed Councils. When they were refused permission to march to City Hall, where they intended to present their demands for relief and unemployment insurance, the demonstrators threw themselves against the massed ranks of mounted and foot police barring their way. It turned into one of the most violent events the city had seen since the Civil War Draft Riots.

By December, 1931, the Unemployed Councils were a national organization which conducted a "Hunger March" of some 1,700 delegates to Washington to present demands for Federal cash assistance and unemployment insurance.

When proposals were made in Congress that the Fish Committee on subversive activities (Representative Hamilton Fish, Jr.) investigate the march, La Guardia, although utterly lacking in sympathy for the Communists, said: "The American home, a steady job, an opportunity for the children to go to school properly nourished, is the way to combat Communism."

The Communists were by no means the only ones to give leadership to the angry protests of the unemployed and the foreclosed. In January, 1932, Father James R. Cox, a Catholic priest of Old St. Patrick's Church in Pittsburgh, led an impressive protest pilgrimage of 15,000 jobless to Washington.

In 1932, the Depression's victims were no longer satisfied

with protest. They began to take direct action. They cared less and less whether their behavior was lawful or not.

In Oklahoma City, unemployed men raided grocery stores and were dispersed by police using tear gas. In Minneapolis and St. Paul, crowds broke into stores and helped themselves to what they needed.

Throughout the great agricultural areas of the Midwest, the Farmers Holiday Association led their members in strikes. Farmers signed pledges not to move any of their livestock, milk, or produce to market until they could get prices that gave them a reasonable chance to keep their farms going. Troops of farmers blockaded the roads and dumped truckloads of food to prevent them from reaching the cities.

When a city family was evicted for nonpayment of rent, the Unemployed Councils took possession of the flat and moved the furniture back in again despite policemen and city marshals.

The foreclosure auctions of farms were attended by farmers carrying shotguns. They went through a grim game of "legitimate" bidding which would end with a top price of perhaps twenty-five cents. As he valued his life, the auctioneer had no choice but to accept the bid. Thus, the foreclosed property would be sold back to the bankrupt owner who would have left the auction homeless and landless if his neighbors had not been there to back up his bid with their shotguns and the terribly calm look on their faces. Sometimes, the farmer had to turn to someone in the crowd to borrow the quarter with which he "bought" back his farm.

To one group of armed farmers who had invaded a Midwestern county seat to stop a foreclosure sale, Fiorello sent a message:

"Fight, farmers, fight! Fight for your homes and your children. Your names will live with Paul Revere's."

The most dramatic and nationally disturbing action of the Depression's victims was the Bonus March of 1932. It started early in May with a group of jobless World War I veterans in Portland, Oregon. Congress had voted an "adjusted compensation" bonus for wartime service, payable in 1945. The veterans couldn't wait that long. They needed it without delay and they intended to petition the Federal Government in person, for passage of Representative Wright Patman's bill to pay the bonus immediately. The three hundred Oregonians who started out under the leadership of ex-sergeant W. W. Waters became twenty thousand from every state in the Union. They camped on the bank of the Anacostia River opposite Capitol Hill. Like the Hunger Marches which preceded it, the Bonus March recalled the image of General Jacob Coxey's ragged army which had colored Fiorello's political outlook in boyhood. Coxey himself had attained the venerable age of seventy-eight and the respectable status of Mayor of Massillon, Ohio. He still advocated Government-financed public works construction to employ the unemployed, but nobody thought it was very radical of him any more.

Unlike Coxey's Army, the Bonus Marchers did not permit themselves to be turned away and dispersed. They remained until June 17, when the Patman Bill was voted down in the Senate. A few thousand left Washington. The majority stuck it out until Congress adjourned, hoping that a new measure on their behalf could be hurried through. They were doomed to disappointment and finally, on July 28, to expulsion from Washington by U. S. Army troops under command of General Douglas MacArthur. Their shelters on the Anacostia River flats were put to the torch. Two veterans had been shot to death by panicky District of Columbia policemen before the Army moved in. One child of a Bonus Marcher's family died of the effects of tear gas used in the onslaught against the veterans.

Through all his postwar years in Washington, Fiorello had been a staunch defender of the veterans' interests. When the Bonus Marchers descended on the capital, he prodded the War Department to provide them with food and shelter. He was sharply critical of the indifference displayed by President Hoover, who steadfastly refused to see any of the Bonus Marchers' spokesmen. When the news reached him that the Army was using tear gas, tanks, and cavalry to drive the veterans out of Washington, Fiorello was beside himself with rage. He drafted a telegram to be sent to the White House:

"Beans is better than bullets and soup is better than gas."

Young Cuneo pointed out the grammatical error, insisting that the message ought to read "Beans *are* better than bullets." La Guardia stormed; "A wise guy. The Capitol in flames and you talk grammar." To the typist on duty he screamed, "Change it! Give the college boy his way." Then, Cuneo recalls, La Guardia stamped his foot and cried "Shame!" stalking into his office unappeased.

Ironically, La Guardia fought against the Patman Bonus Bill because it smacked of special privilege for some of the Depression sufferers. This was his way of refusing to budge one hair's breadth from the idea of direct Federal relief for *all* unemployed workers and auctioned-out farmers. He was aware that his action, six months before election time, might cost him precious votes, but after ten years in Congress he still refused to yield on issues of principle. If people didn't respect his integrity, they didn't need him at all.

The Major's achievements in the Seventy-Second Congress and his ten years as an implacable spokesman for the common man had given him national stature but they turned out to be no guarantee against his defeat in 1932.

The Presidential election year, which offered the people a chance to vote against Hoover and for a Democrat, *any* Democrat, was necessarily a dangerous year for all candidates who bore the Republican label. And Franklin D. Roosevelt wasn't just any Democrat. He was a unique personal and political force. His victory carried a good many lesser candidates into office with him. Certainly his twenty-thousand-vote plurality in the Twentieth was a substantial help to Alderman James J. Lanzetta, Fiorello's Tammany opponent.

Lanzetta was a newcomer to politics, a homegrown East Harlem lawyer of the new generation of Italo-Americans. He took pains to make himself well-known to the voters, as La Guardia did in the years before he won his first Congressional election in Greenwich Village some two decades earlier. Fiorello, on the contrary, was so busy picking up the pieces of the national disaster that he neglected to mend his own political fences. The old Jewish neighborhoods had changed. They were now occupied by thousands of recent settlers from Puerto Rico whose acquaintance and understanding Fiorello had not taken enough trouble to win.

The Tammany machine was tougher, rougher, and readier than it had been for years. Lanzetta's boys smashed store windows harboring La Guardia campaign posters. Marcantonio's Gibboni matched them, window for window. Heads were bashed and votes were stolen by both sides.

Despite the commando efforts of the Gibboni, Marie La Guardia's organizational know-how, and Fiorello's own tireless campaigning, the Lucky Corner turned out, at last, to be not lucky enough. He was defeated by 1,220 votes. But Franklin Delano Roosevelt was victorious by more than seven million.

Politically speaking, La Guardia had nowhere to go for the moment, except to the closing session of the Seventy-Second Congress. There was a consolation prize awaiting him in Washington however—a chance to be an advance skirmisher for Roosevelt's New Deal.

CHAPTER 16

A Meeting of Minds

IT IS NOT RECORDED THAT FIORELLO H. LA GUARDIA, Franklin D. Roosevelt, and James J. Walker were ever together anywhere in the same room at the same time. Yet they confronted each other across the enormous room of American politics in a shifting relationship of alliance and antagonism that moved each of them closer to his destiny.

La Guardia was Walker's junior by a year and a half, and Roosevelt's by six months. He met each of them early in his career.

The first meeting between Fiorello and Jimmy in 1915 was enough to establish the moral gulf that separated them. Deputy Attorney General La Guardia appeared in court as the earnest prosecutor, State Senator Walker as the cynical defender, of meat packers charged with violating a weights and measures law. It was a law which Walker himself had written and put through the State Legislature. Their next meeting was in a patriotic parade through Greenwich Village, the native neighborhood of both men, shortly after the United States entered World War I. The encounter had no special significance except that it was one of the few parades in whch Jimmy Walker ever marched elsewhere than at the head. It was led by La Guardia.

Captain La Guardia, the wartime aviator, and Franklin D. Roosevelt, Assistant Secretary of the Navy, met fleetingly in

Turin while the latter was on an official tour of the European fighting fronts. During the decade after the war, the tall charming patrician and the small explosive immigrants' son saw each other on rare occasions. These meetings usually took place on neutral ground, such as the annual dinner of the Inner Circle, a fraternity of New York reporters who cover the City Hall beat.

Necessarily, the two men went their separate ways. Each bore his own personal burdens. Each blazed his own trail through the political jungles of New York, Albany, and Washington. Each was faithful to his own party, in his fashion. And though their fashions were different, their goals were similar. La Guardia was determined to be his own man politically. So was Roosevelt. La Guardia knew how to play ball with his party bosses and beat them at their own game. So did Roosevelt. Both men were perpetually energized by the ambition to wield their political power for the public good.

When Fiorello ran against Jimmy Walker, who was up for re-election in the 1929 mayoralty contest, Democrat Franklin D. Roosevelt had been Governor of New York State for less than a year. La Guardia's disclosure of the intimate connections between Arnold Rothstein, a prince of the underworld, and the chiefs of Tammany Hall, was the beginning of a serious embarrassment for the Governor. That Rothstein bought and sold favors among the politicians was widely known before he was murdered in 1928; but after his death, the scandalous details began to explode in public, beginning with La Guardia's exposé of the Vitale transaction.

Roosevelt was not yet ready to break with the Tammany machine. The old saying, "I'd rather be right than be president," seemed a little unsophisticated to him. FDR had decided early in his career that he would rather be right *after* he became president. Meanwhile, he played the game of Democratic politics, aristocratically confident that he could do it without getting dirty. He kept himself carefully apart from the growing clamor against the graft, corruption, and irresponsibility of the Walker regime. To offend Tammany could easily have cost him both re-election as governor in 1930 and the presidential nomination in 1932.

Roosevelt took just enough action, therefore, to disarm crit-

ics who accused him of being Tammany's protector. Little by
little, he gave in to the pressure of Republicans, Socialists, clergy-
men, and the newspapers. In 1930, he authorized Judge Samuel
Seabury to investigate the New York City Magistrates Courts.
From every scandal exposed by Seabury there was a clear trail
leading to another one. It became necessary to instruct Judge
Seabury to investigate the office of the New York County District Attorney for its failure to bring hundreds of criminal cases
to trial. Finally, in March, 1931, the Republican State Legislature
succeeded in passing a bill to set up a special committee to investigate the entire government of New York City including the
office of the Mayor. Roosevelt did not welcome the bill but he
signed it and Seabury went to work again. He collected mountains of testimony which demonstrated that the entire city government had been turned into a huge money-making machine to
enrich the Tammany bosses and their supporters. The income of
Judge George W. Olvaney during four and a half years as leader
of Tammany Hall, was reported to have been more than
$2,000,000. Thomas M. Farley, a Tammany District Leader, man-
aged to put $360,000 in the bank during his seven years as Sher-
iff of New York County. Judge Seabury asked him where he got
all that money on a salary and other explainable income that to-
taled only $90,000 during those years. Farley answered that he
kept a "wonderful tin box" at home from which he took money
to deposit in his bank. But he never explained how the money
got *into* his tin box.

"A kind of a magic box?" Seabury asked.

"It was a wonderful box," said Farley.

The phrase, "tin box," became part of the nation's language
overnight, but neither Judge Seabury nor the people of New
York were in any mood for political fairy tales. Mayor Walker
was summoned to appear before the investigating committee in
August, 1931, but he managed to delay his day of reckoning until
the last week of May, 1932.

After a two-day hearing, Judge Seabury drafted a list of
fifteen charges against Walker. They added up to a crushing ac-
cusation of neglecting his responsibilities as mayor, of improper
and illegal conduct, and of giving the investigating committee

dishonest explanations of his behavior. The charges were sent to Governor Roosevelt on June 8, three weeks before the Democratic National Convention. He pondered them for two weeks. On June 22, the day before Walker left for Chicago to attend the convention, Roosevelt put him on notice that he would have to answer the Seabury charges.

Despite the opposition of Tammany, Franklin D. Roosevelt won the Democratic nomination. And now that he had it, he was superbly confident he would know both how to be right and how to be president. In August, Walker appeared before the Governor in Albany, to answer the Seabury charges at a series of eleven hearings. Then, on September 1, one of the wittiest, most lovable and most corrupt mayors New York had ever known sent a brief message to City Clerk Michael J. Cruise: "I hereby resign as Mayor of New York, the same to take effect immediately." Jimmy Walker walked out of City Hall a broken man, leaving behind him a disordered government and a bankrupt treasury.

For almost two decades, La Guardia and Roosevelt had known and respected each other at a distance. The events of the Depression, the collapse of the Hoover regime in Washington and the Walker administration in New York reduced the distance between them. It increased their respect for each other and finally turned them into close political allies.

The alliance began late in the summer of 1932 when La Guardia was invited to dinner by Adolph Augustus Berle, Jr., a man he knew only by reputation. Berle was a professor of law at Columbia University and an authority on economic questions. He lived in an elegant house off Gramercy Park and moved in a circle of statesmen and scholars far removed from the rowdy activities of ordinary politics. Like a few other rich young men of the "goo-goo" persuasion, he had worked among the poor of the lower East Side at the Henry Street Settlement. Now he was becoming known, together with Columbia professors Raymond Moley and Rexford Tugwell and a number of others, as a leading idea man in the Roosevelt campaign.

As a group, these men represented something new in American public life—scholars with excellent executive ability who had developed a strong taste for practical politics. They shortly came to be known as the "Brain Trust." Their task was to provide FDR with a new program of Government action which he could present to the voters—a program which could pull the country out of the downward spin into which it had been steered by the Big Business brains on whom Harding and Hoover had relied. It soon became evident to Fiorello that many New Deal proposals were twin brothers of those he had been making during most of his years in public life.

Marie La Guardia was out of town because of the hot weather and Fiorello went alone to keep his dinner engagement with Berle. The host was a few years younger than the guest; his soft voice and mild blue eyes gave Fiorello no clue to what was on his mind. Berle's quiet courtesy and the dignified splendor of his home contributed little toward putting the Major at his ease. He was automatically suspicious of all rich men. They belonged to the enemy camp because they owned the earth. He was the leader of the meek, who were to inherit it. In his time, he had made allowances and exceptions for rich men who showed a real interest in political reform and he was to make more such allowances in the years to come.

After a few hours of fine food, irreproachable wine, and stimulating conversation, Fiorello added another name to his list of exceptions, and to his list of personal friends. After all, a man who talked about Federal public works, Government subsidized housing, re-employment, and direct relief for the jobless couldn't be all bad. Even when it was time for Fiorello to leave, his host gave him no hint of his reasons for the meeting. He didn't have to. Fiorello was capable of drawing his own conclusions.

That Roosevelt would become president seemed more and more certain during the summer and fall of 1932. In his campaign against Hoover, Roosevelt was pledging himself to a New Deal that would change the quality of Federal Government. Roosevelt proposed the expenditure of vast sums of public money. There would be new restrictions as well as new encouragements for business and new benefits and protections for workers and farmers. To save the country from complete disaster, it would have to be a "radical" program. It would arouse opposi-

tion from powerful financial and industrial leaders who could
not see that what was good for the whole country was also good
for them. Roosevelt would need support from the most able men
he could enlist, in Congress and in every walk of American life.
La Guardia was definitely a New Yorker whom the New Deal
would need, in one capacity or another.

A question that was on many people's minds was what would
happen if a new administration couldn't stop the downward economic plunge. Italy had been in the hands of Mussolini and his
Blackshirts for ten years. In Germany, Hitler and his Brownshirts
were seizing for the reins of government. The United States had
its own varieties of Shirt wearers and would-be *Fuehrers* who
were dreaming of the grandeur of dictatorship. There was more
than the political success of one political party or the other at
stake; American democracy itself was in danger.

The New Deal program simply *had* to succeed, and its be-
ginnings could not wait from the late summer of 1932 until the
inauguration of the new president in March, 1933. The meeting
between La Guardia and Berle was no casual social engagement.
It gave the Brain Truster a chance to decide that the East Harlem
Congressman was the logical House leader of the advance skir-
mishers for the New Deal in the last session of the Hoover Congress. He, if anyone, could prevent that demoralized body from
setting up legislative barriers the New Deal would have to destroy in the march toward national recovery.

By the time Congress convened, La Guardia had almost forgotten his November defeat. He was his old self again, full of
fight and ferocity. With Berle's help, he won passage of an
amendment to the National Bankruptcy Act. This enabled the
courts to prevent farmers and small businessmen from being sum-
marily sold out by creditors. It gave control of railroad reor-
ganizations to the Interstate Commerce Commission, to make
sure that such plans were in the best interests of the public.

Fiorello also introduced a bill for a Federal Farm and Home
Mortgage Relief Bank to refinance mortgages at three per cent
interest for small property owners who faced the loss of their
holdings. Congress adjourned before the bill could be passed, but
a month after Roosevelt took office a similar bill became law.

When Fiorello H. La Guardia left Congress in March, 1933, he was fifty years old. After his five consecutive terms in office, there were still a few colleagues who had not mastered the spelling or pronunciation of his first name. All of them, however, understood quite clearly the political and personal stature of the Little Giant of East Harlem. And if any of New York City's seven million people had doubts about his future as a result of Lanzetta's victory, they were soon to have none.

CHAPTER 17

Here Lies Tammany

WHEN FIORELLO SAW THE NEWSPAPER HEADLINE AN-
nouncing that Jimmy Walker had come to the end of his political
road, he said to Ernest Cuneo, "Ernest, this is a great day for our
country."

It was also a great day for the people of New York City and
for a man to whom they would give their highest honor and their
most unrestrained affection. They would make him their mayor
for three terms totaling twelve years. They would call him "Your
Honor," "The Little Flower," "The Hat," "Butch," or "that little
Napoleon in City Hall." They would riot in front of his home relief bureaus, snarl at his city sales tax, cheer him in Madison
Square Garden, listen to his fatherly lectures on the radio, and
follow him to fires. And they would look back at his administration as a golden age in New York City politics. However, they
did not immediately carry him on their shoulders to City Hall.

Following Jimmy Walker's resignation, Joseph V. McKee,
President of the Board of Aldermen, became Acting Mayor. In
November, 1932, there was a special election for a mayor to complete the remaining year of Walker's term. Despite the disgrace
in which it was floundering, Tammany was able to elect its candidate, Judge John P. O'Brien. No one had anything bad to say
about Mayor O'Brien except that he did whatever Tammany told
him to do. When reporters asked whom he intended to appoint as

Police Commissioner, he replied, "I don't know. I haven't heard yet." He also had a knack for murdering the English language which delighted the newspapers. Reporters were careful to quote his statements exactly as he made them. They were much funnier that way.

The anti-Tammany Democrats, Republicans, Socialists, the unemployed, the labor unions, and the banking institutions to which the City of New York owed some forty million dollars were not amused. Neither were Adolph Berle and his fellow Brain Trusters. New York City, politically, was Roosevelt's home town. It would be a crucial testing ground for his ideas about government and for his methods of combating the Depression. If City Hall were not in capable, honest hands, there could be fatal consequences for the entire New Deal program. It was time for a change in New York, just as it had been time for a change in Washington.

Early in 1933, Adolph Berle and a few other influential individuals concluded that the way to make the change was to organize a Fusion Party. To beat Tammany, the party would need a candidate with an impressive record and with real ability to rebuild the city's ruined government. Berle was convinced that the man for the job was Fiorello H. La Guardia. His problem was to convince the rest of the anti-Tammany forces.

One of Berle's first moves was to arrange a small dinner party. His guests were Mr. and Mrs. Newbold Morris and Mr. and Mrs. Fiorello La Guardia. Morris, member of an old colonial New York family, was the newly elected Republican leader of the rich Fifteenth Manhattan Assembly District, generally known as "the silk stocking district." Before the evening at Berle's home ended, Morris asked Fiorello if he would be willing to address his district Republican club. He was missing a speaker for the next meeting. La Guardia agreed to speak.

Instead of a genteel, slightly drowsy meeting attended by a handful of well-groomed women and men in expensive dinner jackets, the meeting turned out to be something of a political sensation. Many members of the club felt that fighting against Tammany was no excuse for committing the grave social blunder of inviting this uncouth radical. Their protests were given generous space in the newspapers. As a result, the clubhouse was jammed on the night of the meeting with important Republicans from all over New York who had come to watch what would happen.

When La Guardia rose to speak, he looked over his fancy, slightly hostile audience and immediately put them on notice that he had not come to beg for any favors. He began by saying in a low, confidential voice:

"I apologize for being late. Marie, my wife, sent my suit out to be pressed, and it didn't come back until a few minutes ago."

When the audience finished laughing, he continued, "I'm very proud to be here tonight, but I don't know whether you ladies and gentlemen have decided to admit me to the Social Register or whether you just wanted to go slumming with me." Laughter and applause again. Then he took the chip off his shoulder and told them in his most vigorous fashion the facts about Tammany.

The ladies and gentlemen loved it and so did the press. Soon, New York began to think and talk about Fiorello as an important candidate for the mayoral nomination. This was the moment for Berle to talk things over with Judge Seabury, who agreed to become the leader of the Fusion Party. On August 4, there was a meeting of civic leaders and independent members of both political parties at which Judge Seabury and Adolph Berle argued for six hours in favor of a Fusion ticket. The outcome was the nomination of La Guardia as the Republican-Fusion candidate.

Tammany threw O'Brien's hat in the ring for re-election, but Ed Flynn, Democratic boss of the Bronx, had another idea. He decided that two could play at this game of running an independent candidate against the discredited O'Brien. At the suggestion of President Roosevelt, Flynn decided to back the candidacy of Joseph V. McKee who had made an impressive reputation in his few months as Acting Mayor. Naturally, he hoped that the President would speak out publicly at the proper moment on behalf of McKee. But at the "proper moment" Roosevelt remained silent, while Adolph Berle, recognized as an important presidential spokesman, told a large election rally that he considered La Guardia a far more suitable candidate than McKee. Thus, FDR managed to split up the Democratic vote between

O'Brien and McKee, while giving an indirect but powerful boost to La Guardia's candidacy.

La Guardia needed all the help he could get. Tammany was fighting for its life and it fought ferociously. Workingmen were threatened with the loss of their jobs, small businessmen with the loss of their store licenses. Fusion posters were ripped down, speakers heckled, meetings broken up. The Police Department and the private little armies of the big racketeers who did business with Tammany formed a united front to steal the election by fraud and violence.

Nevertheless, the La Guardia forces were cheerful, exuberant, hopeful. Over and over they sang "Who's Afraid of the Big Bad Wolf," which Fiorello had adopted as his campaign song from the Walt Disney film about the Three Little Pigs. Fusion, moreover, was not lacking in money for meeting halls, newspaper advertisements, campaign literature, and radio broadcasts. Nor did it suffer from a great shortage of aggressive muscular manpower to match the Tammany goon squads. The stalwart corps of the East Harlem Gibboni was greatly enlarged by hardfisted flying squads of "Fusioneers" under young Clendenin Ryan. Clen was a son of one of the "Silk Stocking District's" most aristocratic and richest families. Under his direction, Ivy League boxing champions and slum neighborhood Golden Glovers stood shoulder to shoulder against Lucky Luciano's gray-hatted switchblade artists.

Hundreds of volunteer campaign speakers emerged from the mass of New York's aroused electorate to tell the La Guardia story indoors, outdoors, at midday and midnight. La Guardia himself was everywhere. All of New York had become his speaker's stand. He had graduated from his Lucky Corner at 116th Street and Lexington Avenue to Madison Square Garden. For his final campaign rally, the Garden was jammed with twenty thousand listeners while thirty thousand more filled the surrounding streets to hear him over loudspeakers.

On election day, Fiorello and Marie cast their ballots and toured a few voting stations with a group of Fusion campaign leaders and newspapermen. Clen Ryan's college boys and Butch

La Guardia's Gibboni were holding the line everywhere except in several areas of lower Manhattan. A solid platoon of Tammany tough-guys would shoulder their way into polling places. They would tell the uniformed policeman on duty to get lost and drive the legitimate voters and the election officials into the street. One of these hoodlums would sign all the empty spaces in the Board of Elections checklist which showed the votes that had not yet been cast. Another would cast all of these unused votes on the voting machines for the Tammany slate. Anyone who dared to object was beaten into silence. Few dared. From 6:00 A.M. to 5:00 P.M. that day there were eighty-five arrests on charges of illegal voting or false registration. This still left Tammany with a margin of twelve thousand stolen votes, by which it was able to elect Samuel Levy as Borough President and William C. Dodge as District Attorney of Manhattan. Police Commissioner Boland said, however, that it was a peaceful election day, adding cautiously, "for the size of the vote."

It was the largest municipal election turnout New York City had ever produced. The vote was La Guardia, 858,551; McKee, 604,405; O'Brien, 586,100.

In Harlem, the Bronx, the Lower East Side, and Greenwich Village, the Little Flower's triumph was celebrated with bonfires, torch light parades, horn-tooting motorcades, and dancing in the streets. Thousands joined in a jubilant procession behind a hearse and six men who bore a coffin surrounded by signs reading, "Here Lies Tammany—the Big Stiff."

In Times Square, some 200,000 people gathered to watch the election returns flashed by the moving belt of lights girdling the New York Times Tower. As Fiorello's victory became definite, they sang "Who's Afraid of the Big Bad Wolf" over and over again. It was probably one of the silliest songs ever written, but the thousands of voices merging in a tidal wave of sound made it an anthem of vindication and hope for the little people and their furious champion. They had endured four years of the Great Depression. Now they exulted. They had voted themselves a new deal in New York to match the Roosevelt New Deal for the rest of the country.

In Fusion headquarters, Judge Seabury was unruffled by the remarkable victory which he had done so much to make possible. He merely shook hands with his candidate while the newsreel cameras whirred, and said: "Now we have a *mayor!*"

CHAPTER 18

How to Handle a Broom

THE LITTLE FLOWER DIDN'T WAIT FOR THE OFFICIAL solemnities. He started on election night to run the city the way he thought a city should be run. Before his victory became official, but when it was solidly assured, he received a telephone call from Major Arthur B. Cunningham, the Fusion candidate for Comptroller.

"Major," said the other Major, "Tammany Hall is counting me out. My lead has dropped from fifty thousand to four thousand in the last hour. I hear they're holding up the returns from four hundred precincts."

Major Cunningham was new to politics, but the complicated, cold-blooded Tammany vote-juggling was old stuff to Fiorello. He knew that the place to stop it was on the fifth floor of Police Headquarters where the Board of Elections was directing the city-wide count. The two candidates went there without delay. Entering the large noisy chamber, they stood unnoticed for a moment. Then a sudden, horrified hush fell on the shirtsleeved officials and employees. It was as though hundreds of Macbeths had all seen Banquo's ghost at the same instant.

La Guardia barked out short, sharp, angry orders to the police official in charge to send patrol wagons and policemen to all the unreported election districts. They were to bring back the voting machines to Police Headquarters, at gunpoint if necessary.

"I'm going to count those votes for Comptroller myself," he stormed.

When the Board of Elections men saw that La Guardia's orders were going to be carried out, they busied themselves on their telephones. The delayed election returns began to come in and the vote counters went back to their counting under the watchful, angry, dark eyes of their new mayor. When it was over, La Guardia said to Cunningham, "There you are, Arthur. You're elected. Let's go."

Officially, Fiorello H. La Guardia became Mayor of New York City at 12:05 A.M. on Monday, January 1, 1934, when he took the oath of office in the home of Judge Seabury. His old friend and fellow campaigner of the Greenwich Village days, Supreme Court Justice Philip J. McCook, officiated. They knew each other from way back when Fiorello had just launched his unorthodox practice of law for underdogs at prices they could afford. When Justice McCook finished reading the oath, Fiorello replied, "I do solemnly swear," kissed Marie, who was standing at his side, and shook hands with Adolph Berle and his other colleagues.

At the age of fifty-one he was taking on one of the toughest and most important jobs in the United States next to that of president. It was a little tougher for him than for any of his predecessors because he was the first American of Italian immigrant parents to hold such high office.

To reporters and newsreel cameramen who interviewed him in Judge Seabury's library, he said:

"I have just assumed the office of Mayor of the City of New York. The Fusion administration is now in charge of the city. Our theory of municipal government is an experiment to try to show that a nonpartisan, nonpolitical, honest, clean government is possible. If we succeed, I am sure success will be possible in other cities."

Fiorello went to bed late, but he rose early that same morning to begin the work to which he had dedicated himself—the creation of a New York City government which would become a model for cities everywhere. He left his apartment at 109th Street and Fifth Avenue at 8:28, *The New York Times* reported, "wearing his customary wide-brimmed black fedora, a well-used gray overcoat, and a blue serge suit that clung to him with the affection of years of companionship."

He was not accompanied on that ride downtown by any of his prominent political associates but, of all people, by Frank Giordano—Fiorello La Guardia's oldest friend had turned up that morning with something less than a formal invitation. He was there out of friendship. Fiorello welcomed him as a man with whom he could share the kind of comradeship that no Brain Truster, no public personality could give him. On the way to City Hall, simply because it saved time, Fiorello stopped at Police Headquarters in Centre Street and swore in Major General John F. O'Ryan as Police Commissioner in the presence of two hundred ranking officers.

Turning directly to O'Ryan, he said, "Those who are in [the Police Department] through political influence will be removed. Merit will be the basis for promotion. I want you to see, Commissioner, that this message is conveyed to every man in your command."

Ten minutes later he was in the Municipal Building, a massive skyscraper a few blocks from City Hall, swearing in a succession of new commissioners, the heads of the major city departments who, together, would be his "cabinet." Each in turn was told that the new administration would demand efficiency, economy, and complete loyalty to the people of the city rather than to any political party.

After swearing in Paul Blanshard as Commissioner of Accounts, the Mayor said, "I want you to see me as soon as you are through here, I have a job for you to do." The job consisted of several graft investigations which Blanshard launched during his first week as commissioner.

In administering the oath to Corporation Counsel Paul Windels, who had been his manager in his 1919 campaign for President of the Board of Aldermen, La Guardia said, "I don't care whether the law department is the biggest law office in the world; I want it to be the best!"

He told Austin H. MacCormick, new Commissioner of Correction, whose job it was to run the city's jails, that the eyes of the city were on him because he had been chosen from out of town. "You'll have no interference of any kind which, unfortunately, was not true in the case of your predecessor. Your department has been badly mismanaged for a great many years and the institutions are demoralized. Nothing can be lower than for any politician to try to interfere in the administration of a penal institution. They are lower than the inmates."

One of La Guardia's few holdovers from the Tammany years was John MacKenzie, Commissioner of Docks. His work was excellent and honest. To him, the new Mayor's words were: "You had nothing to do with the graft that went on in the Dock Department. All the dirty work happened before it got to the department."

To Dominick Trotta, new Commissioner of Taxes and Assessments, Fiorello gave his marching orders as follows: "There is something wrong in the Tax Department, but I don't know just what it is. See if you can find out."

When Fiorello at last alighted from his limousine at City Hall, he strode across the broad sidewalk and up the steps with Chich following protectively close behind. The reporters streamed after them. To their shouted questions, Fiorello flung back only one sentence, in Italian:

"*È finita la cuccagna!*"

"What does that mean, Mr. Mayor?"

"You'll find out soon enough," he laughed as he entered the building.

Chich turned in the doorway to face the reporters. In his heavily accented English, gesturing eloquently, he explained:

"He says no more free lunch. Finished. The party is ended. No more graft!"

In his office, the Mayor made for his large desk and flung himself into the swivel chair behind it, his feet dangling above the floor. Finding that he had no wastebasket at his side, his Honor commented, "The most important file they had here is missing." He took a moment to examine a tiger skin which had been sent to him by an admirer. It was an amusing present to send to a man who had spent twenty years of his life going after Tammany's hide, even though Tammany had by no means given up the ghost. It had absolute control of the sixty-five-man Board of Aldermen, plus considerable power in the New York State Legislature, which had a good deal to say about New York City's finances.

At 11:15 that morning La Guardia was standing before a microphone in a studio of the National Broadcasting Company to speak directly to the seven million New Yorkers who expected so much from him. The beginning of this new "nonpartisan" administration was a matter of such interest to the whole country that the special forty-five-minute radio program was transmitted from coast to coast.

"Our city, any city in the country, does not belong to any individual or any set of individuals. It belongs to all the people," he said to his listeners. "New York City was restored to the people at one minute after midnight. It is my duty from now on to guard and protect and guide the complete, peaceful, and undisturbed enjoyment of that possession.

"The Golden Rule of this administration is to do after election as it said it would do before election."

What it meant to Fiorello to become mayor, the things he hoped for and would struggle to accomplish, he expressed in that broadcast by repeating a second, unofficial oath of office. It was the pledge taken by the young men of ancient Athens when they attained the age of citizenship:

"We will never bring disgrace to our city by any act of dishonesty or cowardice, nor ever desert our suffering comrades in the ranks. We will fight for the ideals and sacred things of the city, both alone and with many. We will revere and obey the city's laws and do our best to incite a like respect and reverence in those about us who are prone to annul them and set them at naught. We will strive unceasingly to quicken the public's sense of civic duty. And thus, in all ways, we will strive to transmit this city not less but greater, better, and more beautiful than it was transmitted to us."

Returning to City Hall shortly before noon, he received courtesy calls from two former mayors, the bumbling, kindly John P. O'Brien and John F. Hylan, who had been his friend and occasional political ally in the 1920's. Fiorello shook hands, posed for pictures with O'Brien and rushed to the first meeting of the

Board of Aldermen under his administration. He had something important to say to that Tammany body once known in the political lore of New York City as "The Forty Thieves." He didn't mince words:

"You know the city's financial condition makes it necessary to balance the budget. I hope for your co-operation in doing that, but whether I have it or not, the budget must be balanced. I am asking the State Legislature to give me the power to merge city departments and bureaus. That's the only way to balance the budget."

This was not welcome news to the aldermen. It meant cutting out a lot of unnecessary municipal jobs which they had always been able to hand out as rewards to the faithful or to sell "under the table."

"The Federal Government," said the new Mayor, "has promised a twenty-three-million-dollar loan for subways, if we balance the budget by February 1 . . . I make a plea to you now to work together for the welfare of the city. I want to be in a position where we can get that loan from Washington. It will mean thousands of jobs for the unemployed of New York."

After La Guardia withdrew from the chamber, Tim Sullivan of Manhattan took the floor to remind the Fusion administration that Tammany still had considerable muscle. "It is the business of the majority to advance a constructive program," he said, "and the business of the minority to criticize."

When Fiorello heard about Sullivan's speech his comment was: "That depends on who the majority is. In this administration I am the majority."

At 1:15, he swore in Adolph Berle as City Chamberlain. In Tammany times, the job had never amounted to more than that of a glorified financial secretary. Berle found it an ideal position for using his vast knowledge of law and finance to help the city run its complicated system of borrowing, tax collecting, and repayment. Then the Mayor installed his three personal aides, Lester B. Stone, Lawrence B. Dunham, and Clendenin Ryan. After lunch, he dropped into the press room in the basement of City Hall to greet the Association of City Hall Reporters. A few minutes later, they came upstairs for their first news conference with him, in which he again outlined his plans for putting the city government back on its feet.

The Mayor ended his first day in office as he did many of the other days which came after it—at 6:30 in the evening. And what kind of a day had it been, after eight years of Jimmy Walker, Joe McKee, and Judge O'Brien? What was the score after Butch La Guardia's first time at bat?

"With brisk and quiet efficiency, F. H. La Guardia took over control of the city government yesterday," *The New York Times* wrote, "and started at once on the housecleaning through which he hopes to establish a financially sound and well-managed community.

"A new and faster tempo in the administration of the city appeared with him, in marked contrast to the comfortable ease characteristic of Tammany's methods. 'Clean house and clean it thoroughly' was the keynote of the day. Before darkness fell the Mayor had told all his commissioners how he wanted them to handle the broom."

CHAPTER 19

People Eat Every Day

By the time La Guardia became mayor, President Roosevelt's New Deal administration had been at work for nine months. One of its most urgent problems was to devise quick ways to feed, clothe and shelter some twenty-two million people who had lost the means of caring for themselves.

A fund of three billion dollars was distributed by the new Federal Emergency Relief Administration to the cities and states. It became possible to help the unemployed in a more orderly, humane fashion. Families were no longer put out on the street when they couldn't pay their rent. There were fewer breadlines and soup kitchens. The apple sellers disappeared. The manner in which home relief was given and received began to approach the old Salvation Army slogan: "not charity, but a chance."

It was also necessary to *create* several million jobs by distributing $3,300,000,000 of Federal funds to states and cities to build large and small public improvements—dams, bridges, roads, courthouses. The states and cities also contributed large sums for this work. The wages earned on these government jobs and spent by the newly employed, was intended to give American agriculture, industry, and business a massive money transfusion, just as a blood transfusion might be given to an accident victim. It did not put the victim right back on his feet in glowing health, but it gave him a fighting chance for recovery. In fact, the law under which Congress authorized these twin programs of home relief and work relief was known as the National Recovery Act.

In Washington, this vast enterprise was under the direction of Harry Hopkins, an ex-social worker who combined great executive ability with a militant sympathy for the victims of the Depression. Among other things, he had a wonderful impatience with "go slow" plans that would work well "in the long run." His answer to such proposals was, "People don't eat in the long run. They eat every day."

For New York, Mayor La Guardia also chose a social worker, William Hodson, as Welfare Commissioner, to direct the city's relief program. Taking care of the unemployed was a large job. While other cities still fumbled with ways to use the new Federal public works program, La Guardia had begun to blueprint projects that would give employment to thousands. Even before he took office, he had rushed back and forth between Washington and New York to arrange things with Public Works Administrator Harold Ickes. On the draftsmen's tables were plans for the new Sixth Avenue Subway; for a midtown tunnel linking Manhattan and Queens; for new highways; for starting the Triboro Bridge, for schools, hospitals, libraries, parks, and for the city's first municipal airport.

Months before the New Deal worked out laws under which slums could be replaced by building new low-rent housing, La Guardia had set up his own City Housing Authority. Jobless men were put to work tearing down old tenements and clearing sites in preparation for the new projects.

Fiorello chose the arrogant but formidably able Robert Moses as his Parks Commissioner. Moses had less sympathy for the unemployed than his boss did. Both men, in fact, were a little short on sympathy for each other, but they respected each other's abilities. Thus, despite occasional quarrels, the rebuilding of the city's park system under Moses' direction became a key undertaking of New York's work relief program.

At the end of his first six months in City Hall, the Mayor made a report to the people by radio. It was a warm July day. He sat at the microphone in his shirtsleeves, with suspenders exposed, necktie loosened, and completely unabashed by the presence of photographers.

"The city budget of 1934 has been balanced," he said. "In plain English, we saved or raised enough money to make up a tidy sum of thirty-one million dollars and the city is solvent."

Holding in his hand a checklist of promises he had made publicly three months earlier, he delivered a detailed accounting of how he had carried them out.

"You will be interested to know," he purred into the microphone, "that my Commissioner Russell Forbes has just found fifty thousand spare parts of Model T Fords hidden away in one of Tammany's seventy-four city storehouses. Maybe you can figure out why they were bought in the first place."

All at once the voice jumped an octave. "But I can tell you this sort of thing won't happen in Commissioner Forbes' Department of Purchases. We don't have seventy-four warehouses anymore! We've reduced them to thirty-nine and we know what's in every one of them so that we can distribute supplies economically. We save one million dollars on that department alone!

"And I'll tell you something else . . . the six hundred thousand tons of coal we bought this year is *all* coal, not black dust hidden by a thin layer of the real thing on top so that the grafters can get a kickback from the coal dealers."

He reported that municipal institutions had been provided with new staff members. The food given to patients in city hospitals, inmates of jails, and other city institutions was fit to eat now, because the commissary money was being spent honestly.

"We've cleaned out all the parasites and scum from the Sanitation Department. And that ain't a joke. We found the worst demoralization here. Look out into the street in front of your window," he cried. "You'll find it clean now. Do you remember how it used to look? Yes, sir! We sure did clean up the street-cleaning department," the Mayor said cheerfully.

He reminded his listeners that he had cracked down on inspectors who used to demand payoffs from poor peddlers and small shopkeepers. In the Fire Department, three executives now did the work formerly divided among seventeen.

In normal times, all this would have been a considerable achievement in itself. But the Little Flower now went into his report on the relief program. Without political favoritism, 165,000 families were receiving welfare funds. Another 140,000 families had breadwinners on public works projects. The days of selling a vote to Tammany for a basket of food or for a day's work at shoveling snow were over!

The Mayor's accomplishments were so solid that he could afford to understate them somewhat. "The task of running a city of any size in an economical and efficient manner," he told his radio listeners, "is not difficult if the administration has the confidence and support of its people and its press. We have that confidence and that support. We shall carry on."

Fiorello finished the long broadcast in good humor, accepted congratulations from the small group around his desk, and lit the corncob pipe which had become almost as familiar to New Yorkers as his black broad-brimmed hat.

At breakfast the next morning, La Guardia eagerly studied the newspaper comments on his broadcast.

"The restoration of the city's credit is important," said one editorial, "but so is the restoration of morale. Citizens now believe that their government in City Hall is honest. La Guardia has brought about a wonderful transformation."

The Little Flower handed the newspaper across the breakfast table to Marie. "Read this! I wonder just what they expected of me anyway!" he cried. "They didn't think I could do it. Remember?"

Marie ran through the editorial quickly, smiling as she read. She was not misled by her husband's tartness. She knew that nothing could have pleased him more than the words she was reading.

"Well," she said, "you can't really blame anyone for being surprised. It *is* a wonderful transformation!"

The Mayor had not accomplished his miracle single-handedly. Without New Deal funds it would have been impossible to launch any real fight against the Depression in New York City; there would have been little use in talking about civic reform and municipal improvement to hungry, homeless, demoralized citizens.

Fiorello drove himself to the limits of his remarkable endurance and demanded the same tireless devotion to duty from every member of his staff and from all of his commissioners. To keep city employees and officials on their toes, he made surprise visits to city markets, hospitals, police stations, magistrates courts, construction projects, and departmental offices. He placed heavy responsibilities on his officials but kept a close week-to-week check on their work. His commissioners had to consider themselves on twenty-four-hour duty, seven days a week.

Frequently, before his long working day was ended, he reached the point of nervous exhaustion. He would become short tempered, edgy, and sometimes unreasonable with everyone around him.

Once, he ordered a commissioner who was taking a legitimate afternoon off at a Long Island golf course to return to City Hall immediately for a conference. La Guardia was talking to a visitor when the official arrived. He interrupted his conversation and proceeded to give the luckless golfer a lecture on his supposed failure to carry out some important assignment. The commissioner left the office without defending himself but looked greatly puzzled. As La Guardia turned back to his visitor, a shadow of doubt flickered and spread across his face. Then he began to laugh uproariously. Between spasms of laughter, he slapped his desk and shouted, "Oh boy, I bawled out the wrong commissioner!"

Some of his appointees found it very difficult to meet his demands. All of them tried, devotedly, and most of them succeeded. One of them, Major General John F. O'Ryan, who was Police Commissioner, found it impossible. He resigned after long months of conflict about his use of force to break up picket lines and demonstrations of labor unions and unemployed.

The Depression was a period when strikes were numerous in American cities. Wage earners were not lacking in grievances against employers in those days. The unemployed, despite improvements in the home relief system, still felt a desperate need for more generous allotments and less severe regulations. They eagerly followed the lead of organized groups in pressing La Guardia's administration for more relief funds and more jobs on public works projects. Month after month, pickets paraded past City Hall and before the Welfare Department neighborhood bureaus chanting, "Give the bankers home relief. We want jobs!"

The Mayor often grew angry with the unemployed organizations and denounced their leaders. He tried to get strikes settled by reasonable negotiation between the unions and the employers. But basically, he believed that workers who were underpaid and mistreated had a right to strike and picket. As for the unemployed, he could understand their anxiety, impatience, and anger. He felt that the use of police horses and nightsticks against these men and women was intolerable. Once he took occasion to lecture some three thousand policemen on the subject at a meeting in Brooklyn.

"Remember these are hard times," he told them. "We must use forbearance on the men who can't find work. They are depressed. They hate to go home. The unemployed man gets excited. He becomes impatient. With him we must be patient and understanding. Times are bound to be better. It is in the vicious criminal that we have a real police problem. Keep the crooks out of town."

He had a few words on the subject of honesty, too:

"Policemen must recognize that they will always be poor men. You can't get rich in public service. You must learn to live within your means . . . You can usually tell how low the husband is falling by the number of bracelets his wife is wearing."

This admonition came with perfectly good grace from the Mayor. Ever since their marriage, he and Marie had lived simply—in one respect more simply than they wished. They had no children of their own. In 1933, however, they brought a girl and a boy to live with them. One was Jean, the dark-haired niece of the Mayor's first wife; the other was Eric, a blond boy of Swedish parentage. When the La Guardias adopted them legally the following year, Jean was six and Eric almost four. Though the Mayor was intensely fond of them, he permitted the children only rarely to come with him to public ceremonies, such as the laying of cornerstones or City Hall receptions. Despite his interest in publicity, he refused to exploit his children to get it. Instead, he took pains to transmit to Jean and Eric his own passionate regard for the democratic ideas on which the nation was founded. His friend, Newbold Morris, who was then President of the City Council, has written that Fiorello called Eric and Jean into his study every Fourth of July and read the Declaration of Independence to them.

No matter how harsh, angry, or demanding he might have been during his long working day with the army of city officials and employees he commanded, he was tender, playful, and sympathetic with Jean and Eric. He loved children with the special yearning of a man who has lost one of his own. The novelist Fannie Hurst recalled that once when she was accompanying the Mayor to his home, the chauffeur stopped their car in Central Park to repair a flat tire. As they waited, another car stopped and a man got out carrying a child. He introduced himself and explained his intrusion by saying, "I want my child to be able to remember, when he grows up, that he shook the Mayor's hand—that he met Mr. La Guardia."

Fiorello's face lighted up. He reached out his arms, but the child shrank back and began to cry. "Fiorello was sunk," Miss Hurst reported. "His heart was broken. He said, 'My God, children don't like me!' "

It is more likely, however, that the truth was that they adored Fiorello. Someone once said that if children could vote, La Guardia would have been president.

Shortly after he was elected mayor, Fiorello told a meeting of triumphant Fusion-Republican campaign workers:

"My first qualification for this great office is my monumental personal ingratitude." After he was sworn in, he stuck to his determination not to appoint people to city jobs unless they were the best persons available, no matter how hard they had worked for his election. He appointed a few Republican Party officials to city jobs, but he compelled them to relinquish their posts in the party organization. Some people considered General O'Ryan as the first victim of Fiorello's "personal ingratitude" policy. The General had given up his own chance to run for mayor as a Republican in the 1933 election, in favor of La Guardia.

Nevertheless, the Mayor was under constant pressure from

political allies, personal friends, and complete strangers for jobs, privileges, favors. Once when Chich Giordano was sitting in Fiorello's office, an important politician urged certain appointments "for the good of the organization."

Wearily, the Mayor turned to Giordano and asked, "Chich, what do you think you're qualified for? What kind of a job would you like?"

The handsome, gentle barber was startled. He spread his hands wide in a gesture of bewilderment. "Mr. Mayor," he replied, "I don't have the education for a big job. I never ask you for a job. So long as I got a comb and a scissors, I make my living."

The Mayor turned back to the visiting politician. "That's my friend, Giordano," he smiled triumphantly. "That's one of the reasons I love him. He's not always looking to get something for nothing, like a lot of other people I meet."

Not long afterward, however, Giordano was called to the Mayor's office. Despite his desire to be self-reliant, Giordano was unemployed and the Mayor knew it.

"Chich, you're going to work," said the Little Flower peering over the massive black frames of his spectacles. You are now Assistant Property Custodian in the Police Department. You've got to see that lost or stolen property turned in to the police doesn't get lost or stolen again before it gets back to the real owners. I want you to do a good job."

Giordano said "I will do a good job." Then he left to report to one of the Mayor's secretaries to learn the details of his three-thousand-dollar-a-year appointment.

CHAPTER 20

Fiorello Raises a Monument

FIORELLO'S FIRST TERM IN OFFICE STARTED OUT EXPLO-sively. Then it settled down to a steady series of earthquakes, ava-lanches, hurricanes, and thunderstorms. At least, it seemed that way. Actually, the explosion was only a little man in a big black hat directing the world's biggest city in the agonizing process of making itself over. And even his enemies, of whom he made more as he went along, had to admit that he was doing a good job. But what did doing a good job mean during his first four years in City Hall?

It meant restoring the city's credit and building up the treas-ury; cleaning up all the city departments and ridding the city of the "clubhouse loafers" who received paychecks without earn-ing them.

It also meant improving the city's public facilities: subways, bus lines, schools, libraries, playgrounds, parks, roadways, docks, markets, water supply; improving the services to the people: the police, fire, health, welfare, sanitation, public works, and other departments; establishing a humane work and home relief pro-gram, and finding ways to pay for it.

It also meant modernizing the laws under which the city conducted its affairs by drafting a new charter, or city constitu-tion.

And it meant getting re-elected. Not even La Guardia could

hope to finish the tremendous program he had undertaken in a mere four years. Besides, he *liked* being mayor.

Before La Guardia, there were times when bankers who loaned money to the city would wonder if they would ever get it back. They comforted themselves, on the other hand, with as much as five and three quarters per cent interest they were charging, which was very steep in those days. After the La Guardia administration raised the money to pay back the $31,-000,000 the city owed, the interest rate for new loans dropped to three quarters of one per cent. But first there were fourteen weeks of wrangling in Albany, because the State Legislature didn't want any mayor to have too much authority over taxing and spending. Finally, a compromise Economy Bill was passed which enabled Fiorello to start. His most drastic step was to introduce a series of enforced furloughs (days off without pay) for most of the city's 140,000 employees. This was not a popular move. He managed to make people accept it by showing that he was willing to cut his own salary from $29,915 a year, which Mayor O'Brien had been paid, to $25,000. And in May, after the legislature finally passed the Economy Bill, he cut his salary again, to $21,458. Despite massive protests, some of them justified, he abolished 1,063 jobs and thus saved more than $2,250,000.

Meanwhile, Paul Blanshard, Commissioner of Accounts, was doing some heavy housecleaning. His job was to see that the city's money and authority were not misused by employees or officials. He did his job well.

Ninety-four officials were removed or were forced to resign. Twenty of them were convicted by the courts for criminal and expensive misuse of their offices. Court action was also taken against 119 private citizens for cheating the city and 75 of them were found guilty.

La Guardia loved savings, small ones as well as big ones. He boasted that the city's income from the sale of discarded objects and materials, junk, was $284,000 in 1936—almost eleven times as much as the Walker administration collected in 1933.

Commissioner Forbes' Department of Purchase also sold photographic chemicals used to develop X-ray plates in the city hospitals for $6,000 to a company which extracted the silver deposits from them. The department scored such now forgotten triumphs as saving $50,000 a year on the price it paid for fuel oil, $100,000 on printing costs, and $2,700 on electric light bulbs. Forbes' department was in charge of spending about $25,000,000 a year for 60,000 different items. For the hospitals and other city institutions it bought 1,000,000 pounds of butter, almost 9,000,000 quarts of milk, more than 3,500,000 pounds of meat. When Commissioner Forbes' men went to market, no butcher dared to put his thumb on the scale.

Toward the end of his first year, however, Fiorello had to do something he thoroughly hated. He inaugurated a sales tax to raise the tremendous amounts of money the city was obliged to spend for relief of the unemployed. To keep the sales tax as low as possible, he also placed a tax on the incomes of the gas, electric, and telephone companies. The State Legislature did not allow him to impose the local income and inheritance taxes which he wanted.

By these means he managed to raise about $66,000,000 a year for relief purposes. This was added to the huge sums which the Federal Government was providing. The size of the job can be seen from the fact that in 1936 almost half a million people in the city were dependent on work relief, home relief, or both. Fiorello's final verdict on the sales tax was: "It is wholly wrong, except for one thing—it raises money."

Across the whole country, unemployment was still a desperate problem. Part of the Roosevelt administration's answer was the Social Security Act of 1935. The law set up systems of Unemployment Insurance for the jobless and Old-Age Insurance for workers who retired at the age of sixty-five. It also provided Federal funds to help special groups of unemployable people: children of impoverished families, blind people who lacked their own means of support, and those of the aged not eligible for benefits under the new Old-Age Insurance plan.

The Social Security payments were not scheduled to begin for several years, but the new legislation followed the principle for which Fiorello had fought so long—the responsibility of government for the welfare of the nation's working people. "Because it has become increasingly difficult for individuals to

build their own security singlehanded," explained President
Roosevelt, "the Government must now step in and help them lay
the foundation stones, just as Government in the past has helped
to lay the foundation of business and industry." This is what
Fiorello H. La Guardia had been saying during his years in Congress.

Although the New Deal's relief and Social Security program
was helping alleviate the Depression, it had a variety of opponents for a variety of reasons. In New York, the Tammany
Board of Aldermen started an investigation of relief activities in
hopes of embarrassing the La Guardia administration. Among
those questioned by the Aldermen's committee were unemployed
teachers who conducted classes in subjects not usually taught in
the city's schools and colleges. One of the teachers interviewed
was a handicrafts specialist. He explained that his job was to provide a wholesome activity for children on the road to delinquency
by teaching them to make boondoggles. The Aldermen pounced
on this unfamiliar word. Their cunning as campaigners told them
it had the makings of a club with which to beat the Mayor.

"What is a boondoggle?" they asked. The poor teacher
explained that it was a name for belts, lanyards, and similar objects woven of rope or leather strips. His interrogators, however,
succeeded in making him look foolish by asking questions which
ridiculed his job.

Immediately, the word "boondoggle" leaped into national
prominence. It became the word with which the die-hards of
Hooverism hoped to kill Federal spending for work relief projects. The matter became so serious that Raymond Moley,
one of FDR's original Brain Trusters, had to make a radio
speech titled: "Relief is No Laughing Matter." La Guardia continued to work at these problems despite an array of critics who
ranged from absolutely sincere to downright dishonest.

The subway system needed serious attention, too. It had
been deteriorating for fifteen years. The Eighth Avenue subway
lines, started in 1925, ran trains on not more than half of its 177
miles of track. With the twenty-five million dollars he borrowed
from the Federal Government, Fiorello finished it and set it into
full operation. Ground was broken for the new Sixth Avenue

line in 1936, and by the end of La Guardia's second term, in 1941, this line was also finished.

When he ran for re-election in 1937, Fiorello boasted of the achievements of his Parks Commissioner:

"Robert Moses couldn't survive in a Tammany administration for three good reasons: first, he knows his job; second, he is honest; third, he has opinions of his own."

Commissioner Moses used money and manpower brilliantly to lead New York out of its recreational wilderness. The old haphazard system of 141 neglected parks was turned into a unified system of 165 parks, 343 playgrounds, 368 tennis courts, 10 golf courses and 2 large ocean beaches. More than 5,000 acres of park lands were added to the city's holdings; 12 new swimming pools were opened. In one summer, 1936, three quarters of a million children used the pools, free. Some 66,000 trees and almost a million shrubs were planted.

La Guardia took a grim, vindictive delight in tearing down the Central Park Casino and replacing it with a children's playground. The Casino was a big, expensive nightclub and a hangout for Mayor Walker and his "cafe society" pals. It was run as a private business by an operator who rented it from the city. To Fiorello, there was something obscene about having a meeting place for wealthy show-offs in the middle of a park where ordinary people from the overheated sidewalks of New York went to get the feel of grass beneath their feet, to look at swaying treetops, and to eat hard-boiled eggs.

"The Central Park Casino, once a playhouse for playboys, is now a playground for children," he exulted.

In less than four years, the La Guardia administration added some 33 miles of parkway to the city's road system and made 133 acres of swamp and shoreline mud into thirty million dollars worth of usable public land. The administration finished the Triboro Bridge and the Randall's Island Stadium beneath it; the Marine Parkway in Brooklyn and the bridge at the end of it leading to Riis Park in Queens. Plans were drawn for the East River Drive, the Henry Hudson Bridge, and a two-mile tunnel under the New York Bay from Manhattan to Brooklyn.

These projects and many others under the direction of the

Parks Department provided relief jobs for 45,000 men who needed work desperately. But in the years to follow, there would be irony in the Mayor's gleeful comment on what these parkways and bridges would mean to New Yorkers of the future:

"When this mammoth improvement is complete . . . the old cry, 'I wouldn't want to own an automobile in New York,' will be a thing of the past. Driving will again become a pleasure."

No city department remained unswept by the new broom of La Guardia reform. In the Department of Hospitals, there was an end to favoritism for patients and employees with political pull. The standards of medical and nursing practice were greatly improved. A forty-three-million-dollar building program was launched. The capacity of the hospital system was increased by three thousand beds and in 1937 there were plans for adding another four thousand.

Under Tammany, the Department of Licenses was headed by crooks who often permitted other crooks to do business with the people of the city. No one could get a license to run a newsstand without paying from three hundred dollars to seven thousand dollars, depending on the size and location of the stand. People who applied for licenses in the legitimate way, by filling out a form and writing a letter, never heard from the department. Hundreds of such unanswered letters were found tucked away on shelves.

First, the Department of Licenses cleaned house. Then it investigated the used-car dealers, private employment agencies, auctioneers, coal and ice dealers, and other licensed businessmen who cut corners in their dealings with the public.

Earning a dishonest living also became much more difficult for the large-scale racketeers and gamblers. During the 1920's and early 1930's, when bootlegging was a big, almost respectable business, even though it was illegal, the more important hoodlums had little trouble. The wholesale and retail liquor traffic, conducted in violation of the Prohibition laws, produced vast profits for such leading beer barons as Dutch Schultz, Vincent Coll, Frank Costello, Waxey Gordon, Legs Diamond, and dozens of others. As their fortunes grew, they looked for new ways of investing their capital, just as prospering legitimate businessmen do. Those who weren't killed off by their competitors developed new fields of profitable crime. A certain Tootsie Herbert managed to enrich himself by forcing dealers in live poultry to pay him for "protection." Protection from what? Why, from Tootsie Herbert, whose mobsters would destroy the dealer's poultry, and the dealer as well, if he refused to pay.

Dutch Schultz collected an estimated two million dollars a year from restaurant owners and from the unions of restaurant and cafeteria employees by similar methods. Truckers in the garment industry paid tribute to keep their trucks from being turned over and their shipments of clothing from being ruined by acid. Other unions were terrorized and plundered by the gang of Lepke Buchhalter and Gurrah Shapiro.

The Tammany District Attorney of Manhattan, William C. Dodge, was remarkably helpless about all of this. In 1935, however, Governor Lehman appointed Thomas Dewey Special Prosecutor to uncover the facts that would put the racketeers out of business. With La Guardia's backing, Dewey got seventy-one convictions out of seventy-three criminal cases which he brought against loan sharks, slot machine racketeers, gamblers, and "protection" mobs who preyed on businessmen and consumers alike. With a reward of five thousand dollars each being offered for the arrest of Lepke and Gurrah, both of these underworld lords went into hiding, as did ten others of their gang.

Fiorello had always been impressed by the ideas and efforts of such outstanding social workers as Jane Addams, Mary K. Simkhovitch, Lillian D. Wald, and Frances Perkins. In his own Twentieth Congressional District, he had seen the work of Edward Corsi, at Haarlem House. It was natural, therefore, that he would want to improve the way children were treated when they were brought before law enforcement bureaus. This is his own description of the changes he tried to make in the Domestic Relations Court, which handled juvenile offenders:

"The first thing we did was to remove all the dry legal rot from the proceedings in which children were involved, to transform the formidable black-robed judges into symbols of kindly but firm-minded fathers and mothers . . . In other words, it was our purpose to change the Domestic Relations Court from a hall of stone walls, wooden benches, and wooden faces into a humane social agency for the benefit of unfortunate children."

During eight of his twelve years as mayor, La Guardia continued to grapple with two complicated problems that called for the best brains he could assemble. One was unifying the three subway systems. This was a project which had been debated for fifteen years before La Guardia's election. All three systems had been built and were owned by the city. The two older ones were operated by private companies, the Brooklyn-Manhattan Transit and the Interborough Rapid Transit. The Independent System, consisting of the Eighth and Sixth Avenue Lines, was operated by the city's Board of Transportation. Since the BMT and the IRT had been on the verge of bankruptcy for many years, it seemed best to put them out of their misery. Payments of $175,000,000 to the BMT and more than $151,000,-000 to the IRT proved to be an excellent anesthetic. The private owners of the two operating companies felt no pain, but it took La Guardia and his advisors seven years to perform this feat of financial surgery.

The other problem was to draw up a new City Charter. The charter is the basic constitutional law from which the city gets authority to make local laws and to run all of its affairs. The charter governs the powers of the mayor, his department and bureau heads, and the City Council. The old charter, adopted in 1897, was a hodge-podge of some sixteen hundred sections and just as many amendments. Some of its provisions contradicted others. It was so out of date that it included a law stating that "horses, cows, calves, swine and pigs, sheep and goats may not be kept in lodging houses." Fiorello called it "a horse-car charter in an airplane age."

Under the old charter the Board of Aldermen was not a democratically chosen body. In one Manhattan District it took only 6,000 votes to elect an alderman. In another it took five times that many. Yet both aldermen had exactly the same powers. The alderman from one district in Manhattan represented 69,000 residents while an alderman from Queens represented a district of 232,000 residents.

The old charter also prevented the Mayor from cutting out

needless jobs which had been multiplying year after year since 1898. That was the year the five Boroughs of Brooklyn, Queens, Staten Island, Manhattan, and the Bronx were brought together as Greater New York under one city government.

Within this central government, there were secondary borough governments, each with its Borough President and its own borough departments. Fiorello had succeeded in consolidating the Borough park departments under Robert Moses. But in each of the Boroughs there remained, for example, a separate Department of Public Works. One Borough President had two hundred engineers on his staff, enough to do the work for all of New York City. A staff that size put a deep dent in the city's budget. And if a bridge were being built from the Bronx to Manhattan, which Public Works Department was to be in charge—Bronx or Manhattan?

In addition to the Borough Presidents and their collection of departments, each borough was governed by a jumble of elected and appointed county officialdom. Their jobs and titles were leftovers from the days of the early English settlers. Most of these bureaucrats duplicated their officials' work.

Mayor La Guardia was convinced that the city did not need 834 county officials and employees. Almost as soon as he took office, he began to campaign for abolishing most of the county offices. He had three reasons: the municipal government had no control over them; they were costing the city $2,300,000 a year; and they were a source of strength to Tammany.

Paul Blanshard, Commissioner of Accounts, started an investigation of the county offices. He was able to show, among other things, that Hyman Schorenstein, County Commissioner of Records in Brooklyn, had no idea of what his duties were. Worse, he couldn't even spell his own name when Blanshard asked him to do so. But he was collecting a salary of $6,250 a year. He wasn't the only one.

La Guardia crusaded for the elimination of these costly colonial leftovers. In 1935, the voters accepted an amendment to the New York State Constitution giving the New York City government the right to abolish all of the county offices with the exception of County Clerks, District Attorneys, and judges.

The Tammany bosses snickered at Fiorello's victory. It wasn't important so long as they controlled sixty-two of the sixty-five votes in the Board of Aldermen. They didn't see how it could ever be any other way and were confident that the county offices would never be eliminated.

A new charter was being written with the help of such experts as Adolph Berle, Deputy Comptroller Joseph D. McGoldrick, Stanley Isaacs, and such powerful civic organizations as the Citizens Union. It was adopted by a popular referendum of the city's voters in the 1936 national election, in which Franklin D. Roosevelt was elected to his second term as President. Fiorello had little or nothing to do with the actual writing of the charter, but the campaign he made for it in his own ferocious style guaranteed its passage. It went into effect on January 1, 1938, the day Fiorello began his second term as Mayor.

Under the new charter, the old Board of Aldermen was abolished. It was replaced by a City Council elected by means of a complicated but painstakingly democratic voting method called proportional representation. Complicated or not, the new balloting system deprived Tammany of its guaranteed majority in the new body. By the time Fiorello finished his second term, the City Council had voted most of the county government jobs out of existence.

The new charter was not intended to do away with the borough governments but to make them more efficient and economical. It also provided for a City Planning Commission which would be able to work out public improvements for the city as a whole. This would end the old each-borough-for-itself method, which wasted time and money, and often produced "improvements" which were little more than a joke and little less than a disaster.

During his first few months in office, Fiorello spoke at a mass meeting in Hamilton Fish Park, near East Houston Street. While waiting to be introduced, he heard Helen Hall, head of the Henry Street Settlement, describe the inhuman living conditions that prevailed on the Lower East Side. "Here in these tenements," she said, "sleeping babies are bitten by rats in the still hours of the night." The audience of ten thousand muttered its indignation.

The Mayor was indignant, too, but hardly surprised. He knew that such things happen wherever there are slums. He knew that slums were destroyers of human lives. Tuberculosis, the disease that breeds in dank, sunless, tenement flats, had carried off Thea and Fioretta, as it carried off hundreds of others, year after year. Slums were the economic prisons of the underprivileged. A mayor who did not try to get rid of them was a failure. But in this, above all things, Fiorello was determined not to fail!

Six weeks after he took office, and as soon as a new state law would permit him to do so, he set up a New York City Housing Authority. He appointed his Tenement House Commissioner, Langdon W. Post, as chairman. It was the first of its kind in the United States. In many regions, Housing Authorities soon became the standard municipal government machinery for making use of Federal financial help in building low-rent housing projects. A staff of sixteen professionals began studies of the city's housing needs, with the help of eight hundred pages of reports brought in by field investigators hired from among the unemployed.

The first modest achievement of the Housing Authority, aside from tearing down hundreds of old slums, was a development of eight buildings in the block bounded by Second and Third Streets and by Avenue A and First Avenue, in the heart of the dilapidated Lower East Side. The new buildings provided apartments for 122 families who had lived until then in the rat traps that Helen Hall described. For their new, sunlit quarters which looked out on pleasant, tree-shaded courtyards, they paid only $6.05 per room or $24.20 a month for a four-room apartment. The buildings were called, appropriately enough, First Houses.

The dedication ceremony on December 3, 1935, was a historic occasion. The morning was sunny but cold. A speakers' platform was set up at the main entrance of the project. There were rows of folding chairs ranged on the roped-off sidewalk, for officially invited guests. On the platform sat Eleanor Roosevelt, the nation's First Lady, holding a bouquet of yellow flowers presented by a delegation of neighborhood schoolgirls. Sitting with her were Governor Lehman, Parks Commissioner Moses, Senator Wagner, Commissioner Post, and Mayor La Guardia, hunched in his overcoat, proud and impatient.

"I rejoice that a beginning has been made to provide Americans with homes in which it is possible to live decently," said Mrs. Roosevelt.

And Fiorello said, flinging his arms wide: "This—is boon-doggling Exhibit A, and we're proud of it.

"We don't claim to have solved the problem of low-cost housing. This is just a sample of what is being done in our country today. I am glad to tell you that you ain't seen nothing yet . . . Federal funds are available for two other projects . . ."

The two others were the Williamsburg Houses and the Harlem River Houses. The Williamsburg Houses were started in 1937 and finished in 1939 at a cost of almost thirteen million dollars. There were twenty four-story buildings with apartments for 1,622 families, who paid the same modest rents as the tenants of the First Houses. A park, playgrounds, and a new school were also established on these twenty-five acres which had formerly been covered by twelve city blocks of Brooklyn's most miserable tenements. Who had ever heard of poor, low-income families in New York having electric stoves, modern refrigerators, new plumbing, and sunny rooms? The tenants in the Williamsburg Houses had them. So did the 574 families living in the Harlem River Houses, which were built in 1937.

At the laying of the cornerstone of the Williamsburg Houses, Fiorello made a reverent gesture to a man, long dead, who had first confronted New York with the shameful truth about the slum neighborhoods in which generations of the poor had lived, rotted and died. The man was Jacob Riis, a Danish immigrant turned journalist, who in 1890 wrote a book, *How the Other Half Lives*. When Fiorello returned to the United States in 1906, it was still required reading for those who cared about their fellow men. It had made a profound impression on the young La

Guardia. As Mayor, he had a copy of this book placed in the cornerstone.

By the end of La Guardia's first term, ten thousand ex-slum dwellers, adults, youth, children, and old people, were living in self-respecting comfort and decency they had hardly dreamed of a few years earlier. In Fiorello's book, *this* was what it meant to do a good job as mayor.

"If there are any monuments I should like to leave this city," he told a reporter, "they are decent, modern, cheerful houses in the place of the present tenements—houses with windows in every room and a bit of sunshine in every window. And I'm for any step that will hasten achievement of this goal."

Some of the imprints that Fiorello made on the life of New York City have faded or disappeared. But these monuments have remained.

CHAPTER 21

Fiorello Leads the Band

JIMMY WALKER ENDEARED HIMSELF TO SOME VOTERS by his jauntiness, his wit, his personal generosity, and his glamorous associations with the guys and dolls of Broadway. All of these he offered as a substitute for good government and political uprightness. He did it so successfully that there were moments when New York seemed to be nothing more than a vast musical comedy starring James J. Walker, with a cast of millions.

Jimmy Walker was a showman, but the Little Flower practiced a brand of showmanship that made Walker's look amateurish. Fiorello gave New Yorkers the drama of creative government and invited them to be participants as well as spectators.

The Army bandmaster's son loved concerts with a boyish enthusiasm and a politician's natural flair for publicity. He attended performances of the New York Philharmonic and the Metropolitan Opera as frequently and inconspicuously as he could. But there were concerts at which his presence was the main item on the program, with the music as an extra added attraction.

Sitting among an audience of twelve thousand in Brooklyn's Prospect Park one summer night, he was invited to the stage by Conductor Edwin Franko Goldman. Fiorello responded by making a short speech and shouting, "What do you say we give Maestro Goldman a rest and serenade *him* tonight?" Goldman graciously surrendered his baton and the mayor led the band through a rousing rendition of "Stars and Stripes Forever," his arms swinging with fervor and authority. If only his father could have seen him at that moment!

The cheers that greeted the end of his performance had little to do with the music. It was Fiorello, short, fat, and sweat-soaked, on the podium of a free band concert on a hot August night that enthralled them. Mostly everyone in New York knew that he belonged to them and not to the city's high and mighty who summered at South Hampton or Tuxedo Park. The baton he held in his hand was not some slender little stick, borrowed from a musician. It was a symbol of civic leadership and he waved it jubilantly in response to the acclaim of his Prospect Park audience.

Ernest Cuneo recalls another of the Mayor's musical adventures. Fiorello had agreed to conduct the massed Police and Sanitation Department Bands at a special performance in Carnegie Hall. The stage manager came downtown to ask the Mayor for instructions. "Is there any special way you would like me to handle the spotlights for your entrance?" he inquired. "Hell, no," Fiorello replied. "Just treat me like Toscanini." These were the moments of being a mayor that Fiorello loved. There were others.

Fiorello was fascinated by fires. His limousine, which had a folding desk and dictating machine, also had a short-wave radio on which he could hear Police and Fire Department calls. There were standing orders that he should be notified at home, no matter what the hour, of major fires or other public emergencies.

Once Fiorello left a special Board of Estimate meeting over which he was presiding, to rush to a four-alarm fire in Brooklyn. The unconscious fireman whom he saw rescued from one of the four blazing warehouses would have been rescued just as swiftly without him, but Fiorello felt better for being on hand. He couldn't be mayor and not go to fires just as he couldn't command an aviation unit in Italy without flying his own combat missions over the Austrian lines. He just had to participate, personally.

On another occasion, while he was watching a performance in the Radio City Music Hall with City Council President Newbold Morris, a policeman came in and whispered that there was a big fire down the street. They hurried to the scene. Before the engines arrived, Fiorello had disappeared inside the smoke-filled restaurant. The firemen were concerned for the Mayor's safety and annoyed by his presence in the burning building, but no one had the nerve to order him out.

"Smoke continued to billow from the doors and windows," Morris recalled in his book of political reminiscences, *Let the Chips Fall*. "I became genuinely alarmed. Finally, after what seemed an interminable time, La Guardia emerged from the entrance. His clothes were covered with soot. His face was barely recognizable."

What had kept the Mayor in there so long? He had been examining the refrigeration system to see if there was any violation of the building code that might have caused the fire.

"He hadn't trusted the eyesight of the fire battalion chief, a dozen trained fire fighters and experts from the Bureau of Combustibles," Morris commented.

There was another time when he participated in the rescue of two firemen trapped in a basement by the collapse of a burning warehouse wall. Clad in a fireman's hat, rubber coat and boots, he groped his way to the side of the injured men and spoke words of encouragement to them as they were dug out. When he emerged, spectators cried, "Attaboy, Butch!" He loved it.

La Guardia's energy propelled him far beyond the limits of an ordinary mayor's duties into a bewildering variety of public appearances and activities.

If La Guardia had been born fifty years later, he might have been the first mayor of New York to orbit the Earth on his lunch hour.

When hundreds of slot machines, confiscated from racketeers, were being smashed aboard a barge on the East River, Fiorello was there swinging a sledge hammer and shouting to the newsreel cameras, "Let this be notice to the gangsters that they'll be treated just as rough as we're treating their implements here."

He was on hand for the burrowing of tunnels, the groundbreaking of housing projects, the launching of ferry boats, the inauguration of new subway runs, the opening of municipal art exhibitions, the dedication of bridges, libraries, schools, hospitals, health centers, public market buildings. He is probably the only mayor of New York who ever attended a chimney demolition ceremony. The occasion was the clearing of ground at Floyd Bennett Field for a Coast Guard base.

Like mayors before and after him, he welcomed his share of 4-H Club fruit canning champions, trans-Atlantic fliers, and visiting European royalty on the steps of City Hall. Fiorello, who had jeered at Jimmy Walker for being a pal of the playboy Prince of Wales (subsequently the Duke of Windsor), once found himself showing Queen Wilhelmina of the Netherlands through City Hall. She expressed interest in the portraits of austere-looking gentlemen in seventeenth-century dress who obviously had some connection with New York's colonial history.

"Are these your ancestors?" she asked Fiorello.

"No, your Majesty," he replied. "They're *your* ancestors."

Fiorello often found it necessary to travel. He visited distant cities in his capacity as President of the U. S. Conference of Mayors. He commuted to Washington to confer with Federal officials about the expenditure of relief funds. And he flew from one end of the nation to the other making speeches on every conceivable subject. During 1937, he kept more than one hundred speaking engagements, an average of two a week. The occasions he probably welcomed most were high school assemblies or graduation exercises. The minds of the young, not yet trampled into conformity and prejudice, challenged him to talk about his most cherished political ideas and social attitudes. He talked in an adult manner to his teenage audiences.

To five hundred graduates of the Needle Trades High School, he said, "A first-class tailor is worth more to the community than a third-class lawyer."

At a commencement assembly of the High School of Music and Art, he told the graduates, "Italy hasn't produced any good music under Mussolini. I don't know about the art, but I guess it would be grotesque. Under Hitler, Germany has not and will not produce a Wagner or a Beethoven."

Speaking to the first graduating class of Queens College, established with his administration's help, he made a rueful joke: "We started our terms together and my future is as doubtful as yours."

Most of Fiorello's speech-making was done during an era when the world was becoming daily uneasier about the growth of Fascism in Europe and Japan. There were even half a dozen varieties trying to get started on American soil.

During the 1920's, there had been only Mussolini, but it was a carefree decade and Italy seemed far away. Many newspapers, moreover, encouraged their readers to believe that even though Mussolini was a dictator, a man who made the trains to run on time couldn't be all bad.

That La Guardia hated Mussolini and all his works was no secret among Italian-Americans. It was his anti-Fascist stand that elected him New York State Grand Master of the Sons of Italy in 1925. Nevertheless, he did not speak out against Mussolini in public. Instead, he gave up his post after a few months because he did not want to endanger the solidity of the Italian-American vote which kept him in Congress. The anti-Fascists would continue to be pro-La Guardia in any event. But he couldn't afford to let the pro-Fascists become anti-La Guardia. To have done so would have sidetracked him on an issue that seemed remote to New Yorkers until after Adolf Hitler became Chancellor of Germany in 1933 and allied himself with Mussolini.

From that time forward, the gathering world conflict between Fascism and its opponents began to reflect itself more sharply in American life, particularly in New York, where no nation and no political opinion was without some spokesmen. Political and national antagonisms, which were traditional in the American melting pot, lost their somewhat good-natured tone and began to turn vicious and deadly. In some New York neighborhoods they even erupted occasionally in small bursts of violence.

The Mayor warned against this troubled state of the public mind by saying that "the battles of other countries must not be fought out on the streets of our city or in its schools or playgrounds." Nevertheless, he seldom passed up a chance to take a swipe in public at Hitler and the Nazi regime. One of these speeches, in 1937, became an international incident. The occasion was a luncheon of the American Jewish Congress to raise funds to counteract Nazi activity in the United States.

Waiting his turn to speak, Fiorello heard a clergyman who was addressing the gathering say, "I would propose to the Mayor that the World's Fair provide a special building dedicated to religious freedom."

In the course of his own speech, Fiorello replied, "I would add a Chamber of Horrors in which there must be a figure of that Brown Shirt fanatic who is now menacing the peace of the world. The peace of the world is rightly the concern of America."

The German Embassy made a dignified formal protest to the U. S. State Department the same day. The Berlin newspapers were less restrained. They called Fiorello a Jewish ruffian, a protector of gangsters, a criminal disguised as an office holder, a servant of "the international Jewish conspiracy." They taunted him with his Jewish ancestry on his mother's side in the coarse language of Nazi journalism.

Secretary of State Cordell Hull, conveyed the regrets of his government to the government of the German Ambassador. Fiorello, outraged, conveyed his further opinions of Nazism to a press conference at City Hall.

"More than 100,000 men and women have fled from Germany since the Nazi government came into power," he said. "Their only crime is that they love religious and political liberty. Unfortunately there are no living artists who are capable of depicting adequately for a Chamber of Horrors, either the personalities of the Nazi government, Hitler himself, or the type of government he is giving." This seemed to him to cover everything except the matter of his Jewish ancestry. "I never thought I had enough Jewish blood in my veins," he said, "to justify boasting about it."

This time Secretary of State Hull conferred with President Roosevelt. Then he offered his government's regrets to Germany again. Somehow, the furor died down. The Little Flower remained in full anti-Nazi bloom. He allowed himself a sly last word when an official Nazi delegation visited New York shortly afterward. He gave them an escort of Jewish policemen.

As the months passed in 1937, Fiorello and his followers had to face an old familiar fact of political life, that the term of office is no longer for a good mayor than a bad one. And a good mayor has to fight just as hard for re-election as a bad one. Perhaps he has to fight harder, because no mayor can be really good without making some powerful enemies.

After three years of reform rule, the rich respectable Republicans who had backed him against Walker were disenchanted. Fiorello spent too much money on relief and was too nice to labor unions. The active politicians who ran the Republican organization, and some of the Fusionists, were disgruntled because he kept his word about refusing to hand out political favors—even to them. Tammany was hungry and ferocious, because he was choking off its remaining sources of income and influence.

"Nobody wants me but the people," said La Guardia. It was true. They wanted him and they found a way to re-elect him. He had made himself so much a part of New York that any other name following the title of mayor would have had a strange and unpleasant ring. *The New York Times* gave him a reserved endorsement, saying, "The continuance of good government in New York is the issue in the municipal campaign and Mr. La Guardia presents this issue to the people."

A gang-up against him by conservatives and machine politicians was nothing new in Fiorello's life. Try as they might, the Republicans, who had learned to hate him the most, could not prevent him from getting their party's nomination. Tammany, for a change, made a shrewd move. It pressured President Roosevelt into asking Senator Robert F. Wagner, a New Deal stalwart from New York, to run for mayor on the Democratic ticket. He was the only Democrat in town who stood more than a ghost of a chance against the Republican-Fusion New Dealer, La Guardia.

For a time, it seemed as though FDR was going to withhold his support from the Mayor of New York who had campaigned for him in the 1936 presidential election. It would have been a shabby reward for a man who had made the New Deal work so magnificently in New York. But everything came right again in July. Senator Wagner informed the press that he had no intention of running for mayor, because he preferred to remain in Washington. "I am quite satisfied that La Guardia is doing a good job," he said.

Privately, he explained that FDR had merely been going through some elaborate political motions, knowing in advance that the result would not be unfavorable to La Guardia.

"The President laughed when I told him I would not run," Wagner confided. "He told me he had bet three-to-one that I would refuse."

La Guardia, too, could afford to laugh now. Wagner was the only candidate who could have challenged him successfully for the support of the American Labor Party which had been formed in 1936 to help carry New York State for FDR. Without this support, he was sunk. With it, he was confident of winning re-election even over the combined opposition of the two major-party machines. In November, he beat the Democratic candidate, Jeremiah T. Mahoney by 453,000 votes. But even though he had both Republican and Fusion Party backing, he would have lost without the 482,000 votes cast for him on the American Labor Party line of the voting machines. He made history on that election day by becoming the first reform mayor of New York to succeed himself.

CHAPTER 22

Tomorrow and Tomorrow

AFTER THE BRILLIANT ACCOMPLISHMENTS OF HIS FIRST four years as mayor, what more could Fiorello do?

Government is not, after all, a theatrical performance. It is a continuing struggle to keep antagonistic forces in balance. It must satisfy the needs and aspirations of opposing groups of people, not at the expense of one group against the other, but for the common good. Nor is government a machine which works with automatic fairness and honesty once it has been adjusted by some political engineer, whether it be Hoover, Roosevelt, or La Guardia.

Fiorello's second-term task was simply to take up where he had left off; to protect the gains and to make new advances; to run the city for the greatest good of the greatest number.

Unemployment and relief for its victims had not ceased to be a massive problem. In 1938, a million New Yorkers were still dependent on work relief, home relief, and other forms of public assistance. In a speech in San Francisco in September, 1938, Fiorello said, "My relief bill in New York City is ten million dollars a month and I have provided seven million dollars of that, and I am doing it without borrowing but I cannot continue it. Relief is only a temporary solution."

There were more apartment projects to build. There would be still more, for that matter, during his third term. By the time he retired from office, there would be fourteen large public housing developments in operation for seventeen thousand families, with fourteen future projects in the planning stage for another eighteen thousand families.

There were parks, parkways, bridges, tunnels, subways, playgrounds, swimming pools, hospitals and health centers still to be finished, and others to be started.

There were schools to be built, elementary, junior high, and high. Fiorello was particularly proud of having established, in 1936, the High School of Music and Art, which gives advanced training to especially talented young people. It has produced hundreds of distinguished professionals.

Fiorello was passionately convinced that art belongs to the people. He wanted New York to become the world's unrivaled cultural capital. He dreamed, earlier than others, of a place in the city where proud and beautiful buildings would house great orchestras, opera companies, theater troupes, and art galleries. It was a dream that has since been realized, without him, in New York's Lincoln Center. Nevertheless, the Center is indebted to La Guardia's enthusiastic support of the arts during his years as mayor.

Among the forms of work relief developed by the New Deal were projects for writers, artists, musicians, and actors. Conservative politicians and newspaper editorial writers sneered at these projects as "boondoggling." La Guardia looked at them as ways of making New York a happier place to live, a city "where they sing all day and go to the opera at night," as the Marx Brothers once said. He lent his official influence and personal energy to encourage the best work and the largest audiences of which the Federal Arts Projects were capable. Symphony concerts and theatrical productions of great merit, offered at small admission prices, attracted hundreds of thousands of New Yorkers. There were circuses and vaudeville shows, too. Murals were painted on the walls of the city's public buildings, where there had been only dull, meaningless paint or plaster. Artists were allowed to experiment, to develop new ideas, and to enlarge their creative abilities. Whatever opponents of these undertakings may have said at the time, it is now the judgment of thoughtful historians that these projects achieved outstanding results in the theatre, literature, and art.

There were new fields for Fiorello to conquer.

In the mid-1930's most of mankind had never been higher off the ground than it could jump or climb, but airline routes were beginning to crisscross the map of America. As a participant in history's first real aerial warfare and as a peacetime traveler, Fiorello knew that air transport was here to stay. His civic pride and common sense were offended by his city's lack of a large airport. The closest that big passenger planes could come to New York City was Newark, New Jersey.

In 1934, Fiorello dramatized his displeasure by refusing to leave a TWA airline which had picked him up at Chicago and put him down at Newark. He pointed out to airline officials that his ticket plainly said Chicago-New York. After endless arguing and pleading, TWA flew him to Floyd Bennett Field in Brooklyn. It was the beginning of his campaign to put New York on the airmap.

Two years later, the city took over Glenn H. Curtiss Airport, a private landing field, and began to plan the world's largest airlines terminal at North Beach on Flushing Bay. Its size has since then been exceeded by the New York International Airport at Idlewild.

Another two years, September, 1937, to December, 1939, and the giant New York Municipal Airport was finished. The original 105 acres of the site were expanded to 558 acres by millions of cubic yards of cinders and rubbish trucked from nearby Rikers Island on a specially built trestle.

The project consumed one thousand carloads of cement, three million gallons of asphalt, six hundred miles of wire and cable, twenty-five miles of underground piping. Five thousand men worked three shifts a day, except Sundays. Early in 1939 there were as many as twenty-three thousand men on the job at once in an unsuccessful effort to get the field ready by April 30, the opening date of the World's Fair.

As usual, Fiorello was accomplishing two things at once. He was providing jobs for the jobless and creating something of permanent value for the city.

Though the airport was a massive achievement, it was less than perfect. It cost $40,000,000 instead of $28,000,000, estimated earlier. Some of the man-made land area still sinks from time to time because of the softness of the marshland on which it was deposited. Dikes had to be built against abnormally high tides that sometimes flooded the runways. The sinking of the land also created special problems in the maintenance of buildings and fuel pipelines. La Guardia's critics called it Fiorello's Folly. Yet a generation after its completion, it remained one of the nation's largest and busiest airports.

The dedication on October 15, 1939, was attended by 325,000 people. Officially, in accordance with the Mayor's wishes, it was to be called New York Municipal Airport. As he began to speak at the ceremonies, three smoke-writing airplanes high overhead spelled out the message: "Name it La Guardia Airport." The Mayor finished his speech without looking upward.

The campaign to name the airport after him continued for weeks afterward. As a man who prided himself on being an unselfish, though far from humble servant of the people, he found it difficult to accept such an honor. Finally, he compromised. He raised no objection to a resolution of the Board of Estimate which modified the official name to New York Municipal Airport, La Guardia Field, "as a testimonial to the Mayor of our city who conceived the idea of this great airport and who was solely responsible for its development."

Solely responsible? Well, not quite. A man named Franklin D. Roosevelt could take a bow, too, since most of the money was provided by the Federal Government's relief agencies. So could the President's advisors, Harry Hopkins and Harold Ickes and a few others. Without Fiorello, however, the airport might not have been built until a long time later.

If there was any undertaking that fired Fiorello's imagination more than the airport, it was the New York World's Fair of 1939-40. Fairs were not new. They had existed in one form or another since men of the late Stone Age had met to swap flint hatchets for saber-toothed-tiger pelts. World fairs had taken place periodically and tumultuously since the Crystal Palace Exposition of 1851 in London. All of them had been colorful, exuberant, memorable. This was to be the most brilliant of them all. To display the achievements of world civilization was only part of its goal. It would also portray the World of Tomorrow which was to grow from the knowledge, the machinery, and the wealth which man, particularly American man, had accumulated.

The fair also had some rather practical aims. It would stimulate United States trade with the rest of the world; attract visitors with one billion dollars in spending money, and provide thousands of jobs for the seemingly inexhaustible list of the city's idle. To create the two square miles of fair ground not far from North Beach, where La Guardia Airport was being built, millions of cubic yards of ashes and topsoil were transported to fill a low-lying valley. It was another triumph of "boondoggling," accomplished by the picks and shovels of the unemployed, with the help of Federal funds.

From 1935, when it became a certainty, until 1940, when it ended its second season, the World's Fair quickened the pulse of New York life. It tantalized Depression-ridden New Yorkers who had trouble paying the rent. Some dreamed of the Fair as the perfect place for exploiting the brilliant commercial idea they had once had, and of getting wealthy in a few whirlwind months. Almost everyone went, at least once, to let himself be wrapped in the dream of Tomorrow's World which would be so much better than today's. Floods of colored light, fountains, music, clean-looking modern architecture, and the imposing and symbolic Trylon and Perisphere had turned Flushing Meadow into a sea-level Shangri-La. Everyone pushed past the turnstiles expectantly and came out refreshed, or at least bemused.

Attired in striped trousers, a cutaway coat, and top-hat, La Guardia drove to the World's Fair on opening day, April 30, 1939, seated between Franklin and Eleanor Roosevelt. The President made the dedication speech, but a special role remained for the Mayor. He welcomed the world to the Fair's Plaza of the Freedoms. It was a square in which stood massive figures symbolizing the freedoms of the press, religion, assembly, and speech. La Guardia said to his listeners that there must be still another freedom if the first four were to have their fullest meaning:

"There must be economic freedom . . . the right to live decently and happily and to give your children a chance in life . . ."

Before making his address, he felt obliged to change from his ceremonial attire to more informal clothes. "I can't get used to talking about freedom in a cutaway," he explained.

Long before the day they rode to Flushing Meadow together, La Guardia had begun to dream of becoming Roosevelt's successor to the presidency. It was not so wild a dream. He was considered by the President himself, and by other political leaders, as a man of presidential abilities. His long years in Congress and his brilliant record as mayor had made him a nationally known figure. During the 1920's he had been called "America's Most Liberal Congressman." Now he was regarded as "America's Number One Mayor." For four years, the eyes of the nation had been on him, because municipal corruption is a common ailment and American cities are always interested in watching each other try new cures. He was also in the public eye as a leading practitioner of New Deal methods and attitudes for combating the Depression.

Fiorello made the first discreet revelation of his dream late in November, 1937, to Harold Ickes, Secretary of the Interior and Federal Public Works Administrator. They both believed that a powerful effort to dump the New Deal would be made in the 1940 presidential election. There were influential leaders in both parties who wanted the Government to go back to the old Hoover policies of helping Big Business but letting the people shift for themselves.

No one could guess so far in advance that the President would run for a third term. La Guardia felt certain that the Democrats would choose a conservative candidate to succeed Roosevelt. But a liberal candidate who could capture the Republican Party nomination would stand a great chance of being elected, Fiorello thought. This was the strategy the two men discussed at lunch in a Washington restaurant.

"La Guardia believes that the people, generally, will not stand for a return to a reactionary administration," Ickes wrote in his diary. "He thinks that while the people are liberal, there are very few liberal leaders in the country . . . La Guardia said that the kind of candidate the liberals need is a crusader. No names were mentioned, but naturally, the thought occurred to me that perhaps La Guardia regarded himself as the possible crusader that would be required."

All during 1938, Fiorello continued to entertain the hope that he could win either the Republican or a third-party nomination for the presidency. Barring that, he hoped Ickes could become a presidential candidate, and choose him as a vice-presidential running mate.

The Mayor wasted no time in testing these possibilities. Early in the year, he embarked on a series of speaking engagements across the country that made his intentions unmistakable. He was not displeased with the rash of newspaper articles suggesting that he had a presidential bee in his bonnet. But when a reporter questioned him directly about his ambitions, he replied, "A man holding one public office, with his mind on another, is like a driver sitting in a car with a pretty girl at his side—he just can't keep his mind on his work."

Nevertheless, between February and September, 1938, Fiorello found time for an impressive schedule of speaking engagements, which took him west to California and south to Louisiana. He addressed school teachers in Indiana, civil service workers in Michigan, businessmen in Florida, clothing workers in New Jersey, and other organized groups in Tennessee and Texas.

At Guthrie, Oklahoma, he was honored by Indians who made him a member of their tribe and named him Chief Rising Cloud. In his speech of thanks, he said, "We have a great tribe in New York known as Tammany. Any time Oklahoma wants to trade Indians, I have some I will gladly swap."

His visit to San Francisco as the guest of Mayor Rossi was something of a civic celebration. Thousands of admirers lined the sidewalks to greet him as he drove through the main streets in a motorcade at the side of his host. The hills of San Francisco echoed with hurrahs and shouts of "Attaboy, Fiorello."

In Los Angeles, where he addressed an audience of five thousand in the Shrine Auditorium, he was introduced by Eddie Cantor as "that outstanding animal trainer, the man who, singlehanded, vanquished the snarling Tammany Tiger." Another speaker, referring to the fact that Los Angeles had just chosen a new mayor, said, "Mayor La Guardia has set us the example and has shown that an honest man can overcome corrupt government."

In his year of following the presidential dream across the continent, there was no moment that stirred him more than his visit to Prescott, the sun-baked little city he called his home town.

It was his second homecoming in four years. In 1935, he returned to Prescott after a thirty-seven-year absence to receive a rousing public welcome as a native son who made good in the nation's Big City. Fiorello wore a cowpuncher's hat and shook hands with Joe Bauer, an old bare-knuckles adversary of his grammar school days. Unsuccessfully, he looked for the old Goldwater general store and had lunch in the Chinese restaurant he had known only from the outside during the 1890's.

In 1938, it was Auld Lang Syne Day again, bigger than before. Early in the morning, he drove to Prescott from Phoenix in an open car, sniffing the air for familiar scents and scanning the landscape for the scenes of his childhood. On the outskirts of town, he was presented with a cow pony and a ten-gallon hat. He rode into town in a cavalcade of old-timers, the high school band bringing up the rear.

He dismounted at the courthouse where he had once loitered to hear his hero, Bucky O'Neill, hold forth on the issues of the day. As he stood at the top of the steps to greet Prescott, he was aware of the O'Neill memorial which had been erected in the square.

One of the boyhood friends who gathered at breakfast to swap yarns with him brought an old two-foot ship model which had been carved for Fiorello by a soldier at Whipple Barracks. Later in the morning Fiorello spoke to the student body at Prescott High School and (how could he resist the opportunity?) led the school band.

In the afternoon, a throng of townspeople gathered at Granite Dells, an area of picturesque rock formations, for a ceremony in which the highest outcropping was named Point La Guardia, in honor of Achille. Fiorello drove to the Dells giving Marie a guided tour of the Prescott countryside as they went.

"This is one of the happiest days of my life," he said to the gathering. "Those who knew my father remember him for his kindness and thoughtfulness. I shall remember this occasion all of my life." He meant it.

CHAPTER 23

End of a Dream

THE MAGNIFICENT WORLD'S FAIR WAS A POETIC FORE-cast of enduring peace and plenty in the decades to come, yet seldom had mankind's future looked gloomier than it did in 1939.

Germany was not represented, nor was there the "chamber of horrors" Fiorello proposed two years earlier. Nevertheless, Germany was on everyone's mind. There was a growing horror of what *Der Fuehrer*, his Italian junior partner, Mussolini, and their Japanese military associates might do next.

In the years since 1936, these three countries had made war a familiar agony on three continents. Japan had completed its conquest of Manchuria, begun in 1931, and was pushing farther south and west in China. Italy had conquered Ethiopia and, together with Germany, had given Francisco Franco the military strength to make himself dictator of Spain. Less than a month before Fiorello spoke about freedom at Flushing Meadows, Nazi troops had occupied all of Czechoslovakia. An Italian army had overrun Albania. Before the Fair ended its first season, World War II had begun. The Soviet Union, friendless among the world's governments, signed an uneasy nonaggression treaty with Hitler's Germany, self-proclaimed global leader of the anti-Communist forces. Thus comforted, the Nazis blitzed their way across Poland. Soviet troops marched in from the east to make sure that Hitler knew where to stop.

To Roosevelt and other Government leaders, the pattern of world events was clear. By the beginning of 1940, FDR put an end to his inner doubts about running for a third term. He was convinced that no other liberal candidate, La Guardia included, could be sure of winning. A conservative president, he feared, would become the captive of those who were not seriously alarmed by Hitler's trampling of weaker European nations. He understood that just as he had fought for the New Deal, he must now take leadership in the fight to stop the Berlin-Rome-Tokyo alliance from overrunning the world.

Reluctantly, La Guardia came to the same conclusion. America's insecure position in a world at war and the President's great political skill, made it likely that Roosevelt would be drafted for a third term. In January, 1940, Roosevelt asked Congress for extraordinary peacetime authority to start a costly build-up of the Navy. Fiorello cast aside his twenty-year stand as a pacifist and gave public support to the President's military preparedness program.

During the months that followed, the "Third Term" became a national controversy. No President had ever held the office three times. Roosevelt's political enemies accused him of wanting to be a dictator, but Fiorello told a convention of clothing workers in May:

"As far as I'm concerned, under the conditions existing today, if Franklin Roosevelt decides to run for president, I am going to vote for him."

Fiorello's statement was received with cheers. The common people, among whom there were still more than eight million unemployed, had no fear that a third term would turn FDR into a dictator.

In July, the Democratic convention in Chicago nominated Roosevelt. His Republican opponent, Wendell L. Willkie, was a youthful, energetic newcomer to politics. He proved to be a far more impressive contender than Alfred Landon had been in 1936. Willkie's public speaking technique and personal manner were unpretentious, vigorous, direct. He had an Indiana twang and a lock of black hair that kept flopping down over one eye. He had enough charm, in short, to make his listeners forget he had ever been President of Commonwealth & Southern, a powerful group of public utilities corporations. The odd combination of Willkie's grass-roots style and Big Business background caused Harold Ickes to call him "the barefoot lawyer from Wall Street."

Fiorello campaigned for FDR without letup. He lost no chance to remind New Yorkers that the New Deal was the source of most of the public improvements the city had gained in the preceding years. At every inauguration, dedication, ground-breaking, or cornerstone laying, he hammered home the message that the New Deal was responsible for the Belt Parkway, the eight-story Joan of Arc Junior High School, the East River Houses, with its twenty-nine buildings, comprising 1,170 apartments—for the hundreds of other contributions to the city's advancement.

At the unveiling of the murals created by WPA artists in the marble halls of the New York Public Library, the Mayor stood in the center of the lofty main concourse bending backward and looking upward. Pointing toward the painted portrayals of man's endless search for knowledge, wisdom, and well-being, Fiorello exclaimed, "When all the detractors of President Roosevelt are long forgotten, these murals will still be here."

There were times when La Guardia spoke longingly of a life free from the cares of public office, but that was just an over-worked man's daydream. In September, Congress passed a peacetime Selective Service Bill. Then the United States and Canada set up a joint defense plan, and FDR appointed Fiorello chairman of the American section.

The angry mood of the world was matched by the little Mayor's own explosive temper. There were times when he was downright brutal to his staff and to strangers. He came into his office one morning to find a well-dressed young woman seated near his desk. She had no appointment. The Mayor stared at her in angry amazement.

"How did you get here?" he demanded. Without waiting for an answer, he flung open the door and screamed to a secretary, "What the hell is this woman doing here?" No one knew. The woman refused to leave until the Mayor agreed to listen to her.

"I live with my brother and my mother," the woman explained. "We are out of work and my mother is ill. We've gotten along without relief until now but I've got to get a job. We don't want to live on relief."

As the woman sat trying to choke back her tears, Fiorello motioned dejectedly to an aide who was standing by. "Get her out of here," he ordered, "but do something for her!"

The Mayor's campaigning for FDR produced the usual crop of rumors about political deals between the candidate and his leading supporters. Returning from a conference with the President, Fiorello announced to reporters that he had used his personal influence to get his old political enemy, James J. Walker, a job at twenty thousand dollars as chief mediator of labor-management disputes in the garment industry. A reporter asked Fiorello, "Why did you do it, Mr. Mayor?"

"The man has to live," he retorted. "He's down and out."

The anti-Roosevelt newspapers, that is to say, most of them, did not interpret La Guardia's deed as charity toward a beaten adversary. They hinted that it was a piece of political horse trading by which Fiorello hoped to ensure his chances of an important appointment in Roosevelt's third-term administration.

The fact is that, for a while, FDR had considered making Fiorello Secretary of War. The appointment finally went to Henry L. Stimson because important Democrats considered Fiorello to be politically too "far out."

As election day drew nearer, the guessing game among the reporters grew hotter. They persisted in their questions to the Mayor about the kind of job he expected from FDR. Fiorello either laughed off the questions or snarled with anger, depending on his mood. They enjoyed the game, however, because it put the aggressive little Mayor on the defensive. Many of the members of the working press were less than charitable toward Fiorello, because he often managed to treat them rather highhandedly. They felt that for a man who knew the value of publicity and had remarkable skill in manipulating the power of the press, he was not sufficiently fond of reporters. What disturbed them most was his quick, fierce resentment of almost any kind of criticism.

Irving Spiegel, a veteran staff member of *The New York Times*, recalls that after covering a speech by La Guardia in the Bronx, he approached the Mayor to ask him a question. In the course of the conversation which followed, Fiorello said, "Well, Irving, what did you think of my speech?"

"It was a fine speech," Spiegel replied. "Lots of substance. But there was one place where I thought your voice rose too high."

The Mayor glowered at the young reporter and said: "I was going to give you a lift downtown in my car, but now you're on your own." Spiegel rode back to Times Square on a subway train.

On Election Day, 1940, Fiorello toured the city to see for himself that there was no deception at the polls. There wasn't any to speak of. By ten o'clock that night, he knew that Roosevelt had won. He also knew, by simple political intuition, that he had lost his chances of ever being president or of playing an important role in FDR's third-term administration. The reporters wouldn't let up, however. The following morning, at City Hall, they confronted him with still another version of the same old question: "Mr. Mayor, are you in line for an appointment in Washington?"

Fiorello didn't even try to keep his temper. "I can understand that question," he shrilled. "It is prompted by the corporation mentality which just assumes that everything was bought and paid for in this campaign." He lapsed into silence long enough to recover his dignity. Then he said, "If my country is in trouble, I'll do anything that is asked of me."

CHAPTER 24

"Patience and Fortitude!"

ON FLUSHING MEADOW, WORKMEN WERE DISMANTLING the World of Tomorrow. In Europe, the Nazis were tearing down yesterday's civilization. And in City Hall, Fiorello La Guardia contemplated the uncertain shape of his immediate future. It was uncertain because the future of the whole world was in doubt.

In March, 1941, President Roosevelt made a speech that spelled out the changes World War II was making in the nation's activities and in its destiny. "The British people and their allies need ships," he said. "From America they will get ships. They need planes. From America they will get planes. They need food . . . They need tanks and guns and ammunition and supplies of all kinds. From America they will get tanks and guns and ammunition and supplies of all kinds . . . Our country is going to be what our people have proclaimed it must be—the arsenal of democracy."

Though not at war, the United States was enlarging its army, navy, and air force. The peacetime draft took a million men out of the competition for civilian jobs and created an urgent demand for the war goods that the armies of Europe and Asia needed, plus a little more.

By August, 1941, the national total of unemployed dropped to five and one-half million, the lowest figure in ten years. Farmers no longer plowed their corn and cotton back into the ground nor slaughtered their livestock to keep it off the market. Factories hung out "Help Wanted" signs. New York City's industries also became part of the busy arsenal of democracy. Vast amounts of the nation's new production was flowing into the city for shipment to the European nations whose own farms and factories were being overtaxed or destroyed.

Thus, war and the preparation for war were accomplishing almost overnight what private industry and Government had been unable to achieve in the years after 1929. War was putting an end to the Great Depression.

Most Americans who had lived through that desperate decade could see nothing terrible in the destructive nature of the prosperity they were beginning to enjoy. They had decent human regrets about the events overseas. They hoped that once Fascism had been crushed, they could live the dream of the World of Tomorrow. Meanwhile, a job in a bayonet factory was a welcome change from the begging, borrowing, and worrying of the 1930's.

All of this made the New York of 1941 different from the bedraggled, floundering city Fiorello had undertaken to lead in 1934. The mood of desperation and anger had almost vanished. The unemployment relief demonstrations gave way to demonstrations in favor of keeping out of the war or of entering it. The crowds, on either side of the issue, were made up of the formerly unemployed and the about-to-be employed. Collections for the jobless were replaced by solicitations for Bundles for Britain. The rich ladies who had worked among the poor in the Depression were wearing the quasi-military uniforms of the American Women's Voluntary Services. They were driving station wagons, helping the Red Cross collect blood, and handing out doughnuts in servicemen's canteens on Broadway where there had once been soup kitchens.

As the early months of 1941 slipped by, it became apparent that the United States, sooner or later, would go to war. But still, Fiorello had no sign as to what was going to be his role in it. There was no clarion call from Washington to join the White House team.

Although FDR had appointed him Director of the newly-created Office of Civilian Defense and had made him Chairman of the United States section of the Joint Permanent United States-Canadian Defense Board, in a way, these titles were worse than no White House recognition at all. They would only keep him on the edge of the tremendous struggle into which the nation was moving, step by step. Fiorello didn't like being on the edges of anything. He wanted, always, to be *in* action, not *near* it.

The shifting of huge Government funds from public works to the military establishment foreshadowed the end of his heroic efforts to rebuild New York. His dream of a city that would dazzle all the world, with its physical beauty, moral vigor, and cultural attainments was rapidly coming to an end. From now on, the job of mayor would make him not a planner and a creator, but a caretaker and a paper-shuffler. In his distaste for legalistic caution and administrative detail, he once cried out, in print:

"Let's go! For God's sake, leave out the commas, the semicolons, and the rest of that lawyer stuff. Get down to the guts of the thing—what does it really mean?" Watching semicolons wasn't his kind of action. But where was there any other kind?

Reluctantly, he stopped looking toward Washington. World events had trapped him into running for a third term, and if the rest of the country didn't need him, New York certainly did. Once again, the Little Flower put his vote-getting abilities to the test under the joint banner of the Republican, American Labor, and City Fusion Parties. Despite the protests of the New York Democrats, President Roosevelt gave Fiorello his unreserved public endorsement:

"I do not hesitate to express the opinion that Mayor La Guardia and his administration have given to the city the most honest and, I believe, the most efficient municipal government of any within my recollection."

The Democrats felt they had been betrayed. They campaigned against Fiorello with a ferocity that expressed their lust for vengeance. They spent almost as much time and energy defaming the Little Flower as they did proclaiming the virtues of William O'Dwyer, their own candidate. O'Dwyer was fifty, eight years younger than La Guardia. In the thirty years since he had come to New York from Ireland, he had been a hod carrier, clerk, plasterer, bartender, policeman, lawyer, and judge. As a gangbusting District Attorney of Brooklyn, he had built a substantial reputation by smashing the criminal fraternity known as Murder, Inc.

Fiorello campaigned with much of his old vigor and shrewdness, but the joy of battle was not in him, except when he could taunt the desperate Democratic leaders.

In a single statement, he disposed of three of them, Frank V. Kelly, of Brooklyn; Christopher Sullivan, head of Tammany; and Edward J. Flynn, of the Bronx:

"The Flynn-Kelly-Sullivan machine believes that the boys are entitled to loot every now and then. Why, they haven't had a chance to earn a dishonest living in eight years. 'Grabby' Kelly doesn't know anything about the city. 'Parlay' Sullivan, all he knows about the city is Belmont, Aqueduct, and Empire [race tracks]. He picks his horses like he picks his candidates—losers. Ed Flynn, he has an air of respectability. He has no spots on his vest. He wears a tux at times, but he is just a political boss, interested only in the political philosophy of spoils and loot."

It was a fairly dull campaign. Everyone took it for granted that La Guardia would be re-elected. However, Fiorello was comforted by one campaign event which was as much personal as it was political. This was his reconciliation with Vito Marcantonio. They had drifted apart during 1939 and 1940 because of their sharp differences about the war and American foreign policy.

At the time of their first association in 1924, Fiorello, who had just lost his wife and child, told his partners in the law firm of Foster, La Guardia and Cutler, "I want to make him my professional heir." Accordingly, he kept a stern but affectionate eye on Marc and put him to work in the firm when he was graduated from New York University Law School. When Marc set up his own office, Fiorello became his partner for a short time and went out of his way, later, to help his protégé build up his practice.

When Fiorello wrote to Marc from Washington, he addressed him as "Dear Sonny," and in at least one such letter, he delivered a paternal lecture to the then twenty-two-year-old Marcantonio:

".. . You have an opportunity such as very few boys have, other than those who can step into their own father's office and know that one day it will be theirs. That is what I am offering you . . . If you love your profession, want to be proficient in it, and intend to follow it, then you have got to change your attitude and your whole mode of living. You have to cut out your evening appointments, your dances, your midnight philosophers for the next five years and devote yourself to serious hard study of the law. From 1907 to 1912 I did it . . .

"Be careful in your personal appearance. Get a Gillette razor and keep yourself well-groomed at all times. Be always respectful and courteous to all, the humble as well as the high, and for goodness sake, keep your ears and eyes open and keep your mouth closed for at least the next twenty years.

"Now my dear boy, take this letter in the fatherly spirit that I am writing it. Keep in touch with me."

With the advice and help from Fiorello, his own abilities, and his fierce devotion to the little people of his native neighborhood, Marcantonio seemed ready to follow in La Guardia's footsteps in Congress. Marcantonio represented East Harlem for fourteen years, despite Tammany-Republican coalitions and changes in the boundaries of his Congressional District designed to outnumber his supporters. Few men have ever been repeatedly elected to Congress from the same district in the face of such powerful opposition. (He affiliated himself with the American Labor Party from the first, and was one of the organizers with Fiorello in 1936. In November, 1938, Marc was elected to Congress as the only American Labor Party member, after having also won the Republican nomination.)

As the years sped by, Fiorello found deep personal satisfaction in the rise of Vito Marcantonio. But the independence of mind and moral courage which they so much admired in each other opened a temporary gulf between them.

In 1940, Representative Marcantonio cast the only vote in the House against FDR's greatly expanded military budget. He opposed the peacetime draft and placed himself on the side of those who demanded that the United States remain strictly neutral, while Fiorello, for the second time in his public life, followed a president along a path that would lead to war.

By the middle of 1941, with large areas of Western Europe occupied by the Nazis and fresh Hitler legions rolling across Russia, even the neutralists became alarmed. Some of them were pro-New Deal like Marcantonio; others were Roosevelt-hating anti-New Dealers. Most of them began to see that the United States might be left standing alone to defend itself in a world conquered by the Hitler-Mussolini-Hirohito Axis. Marcantonio, like many others, reversed his stand and announced his wholehearted support of President Roosevelt's foreign policy.

Though they had remained uneasy political allies of a sort during 1940 and part of 1941, Fiorello's campaign for re-election rekindled the warmth of their personal friendship. In the final outdoor meeting at the Lucky Corner, before an audience of 25,000, Marc sailed into the Mayor's opponents in his best foot-stamping, arm-waving style. Everyone was wearing a button bearing the legend, "Call Me Butch" and Fiorello knew, as his eyes roved over the crowd, that they would call him Mayor again.

On Election Day, he behaved with less than his usual zest for battle. He spent part of the day sitting alone in a sea of empty seats at Carnegie Hall, where Bruno Walter was conducting a rehearsal of the New York Philharmonic. Unsoothed by the darkness and tranquility of the concert hall, Fiorello went out again to the election. Before midnight, he knew that he had defeated O'Dwyer, but only by a small margin of 132,000 votes.

In the idle, sunless Sunday afternoon of December 7, 1941, New York learned that the Japanese bombers had attacked Pearl Harbor. The next day the United States was officially at war, allied with England, France, the Soviet Union, and all the nations of two hemispheres who were struggling against Axis oppression.

Immediately, La Guardia's third term took on a new meaning. New York was not only the world's largest city, it was its biggest military seaport, sending goods to mankind's most murderous and destructive war. It was the great chute through which the boundless output of democracy's arsenal flowed overseas to the battlefronts.

In the months since his appointment by FDR, Fiorello found that he and the Office of Civilian Defense were not suited to each other. It was the one job in his whole career which he did not handle successfully. Besides, his work as director was interfering more and more with his duties as wartime mayor. He resigned his directorship in February, 1942.

During the Depression years, Fiorello had taken the lead in creating jobs for the unemployed and settling labor disputes. Now, it became one of his chief concerns to find people for the wartime jobs that remained unfilled. Students were leaving the high schools because factories and offices were offering salaries that seemed handsome to teen-agers who had grown up on relief.

Girls and women found a new freedom in the wartime industries of New York and the rest of the nation. They went to work in slacks and overalls. They learned to handle noisy, dirty, complicated, machinery and proved their equality with men on the assembly lines.

The quick and turbulent changes in the life of the city confronted the La Guardia administration with new, unfamiliar problems. Nursery centers had to be set up for the children of women who went to work in defense plants. The gains La Guardia had made in low-rent housing were being wiped out by an influx of new residents and by the shortage of building materials and labor.

Emergency Federal price and rent control laws were passed to prevent the cost of living from running wild. Enforcement was up to the local authorities in each community. In New York City, Fiorello enforced these laws effectively. He had to maneuver and negotiate to protect the city against unexpected shortages of fuel and food. The city's water supply and electric power plants had to be protected against the possibility of sabotage.

Gasoline and rubber tires were rationed. Car pools became common and Sunday driving for pleasure was a thing of the past. For the duration of the war, the Mayor stored his big official limousine and drove a small black coupe to cut down on gasoline consumption.

Fiorello did not want the city to be caught napping by the enemy. He insisted that practical measures be taken for civilian defense against the possibility of token air raids by Nazi bombers. He organized his own "war cabinet" declaring, "The City Charter makes me responsible for the safety of the inhabitants of New York." He set up a widespread system of air raid wardens, emergency fire fighting crews, demolition, rescue and decontamination squads, and emergency medical units.

His critics poked fun at him; most New Yorkers didn't worry about the possibility that Nazi planes might bomb New York. Nevertheless, after many confused and ineffectual practice air raid alerts in various neighborhoods, the first city-wide blackout test was conducted at nine-thirty on a midsummer night in 1942. The Mayor, Fire Commissioner Walsh, and Police Commissioner Valentine took their post on the roof of the Empire State Building, 102 stories above Fifth Avenue and waited nervously. Would the people respond? Or would they go their way and make La Guardia's civilian defense program a national joke in the next day's newspapers?

The sirens wailed and within minutes there was nothing but darkness. The Mayor gasped as New York blotted itself out before his eyes. Something else was gone—the roar of the city's nighttime traffic. Streetcars, buses, elevated trains, trucks, taxis, had come to a halt. Where there had been a giant city, brightly lighted and noisy, there was nothing now but a black and silent void. It is possible that for a moment Fiorello might have felt as though he had willed an un-Creation.

The event helped to restore the Mayor's flagging spirits. Only the willing co-operation of New York's millions could have made the blackout test so successful. The people, it appeared, had not ceased to take "Butch" seriously.

The city also listened earnestly, affectionately, and with appreciative amusement, to his Sunday-at-noon "Talks to the People." The series, begun two weeks after Pearl Harbor on WNYC, the municipal radio station, continued without interruption until the end of his term in 1945. Fiorello was an old hand at the microphone. Next to FDR, he was probably the nation's most appealing radio personality in political life.

The opening and closing signature of the broadcasts was "The Marines' Hymn." After the announcer's introduction, Fiorello, seated at his desk, with a folder of documents and newspaper clippings at hand, would salute his listeners with the words: "Patience and fortitude!"

"Remember?" he would begin. "I told you last week that lamb would be plentiful and all you had to do was to sit tight and not buy and the price would come down? The gates of the penitentiary must be opened for those who violate the rationing and price control system. The bootlegger of Prohibition days was an ethical businessman compared to the black market operator.

"Well, you know the black market was forced to sell at ceiling prices because you listened to me and wouldn't buy lamb last week. We struck where it hurts most, right in their perishable stocks. Ha! ha! ha!" His listeners could hear the sound of his fist thumping his desk with satisfaction.

"I suppose if you ask some prosperous Italians around town, 'Do you know what *pasta-fagioli* is?' they'll say, 'O-o-o-oh, No-o-o-o, we never heard of it at our house.' That's a lot of bunk. All poor people eat it, but nowadays it's quite a luxury and very nutritious. It has proteins, vitamins, starch—and no ration stamps required!" Then he would proceed to read Marie's own recipe for the dish.

His radio talks were no substitute for unending personal appearances to launch drives for war-supporting activities—the sale of war savings bonds, blood donation campaigns, and waste paper, rag, and metal scrap collections.

The Little Flower also found time to make secret shortwave broadcasts to Italy for the State Department. He fanned the hatred against Mussolini and Hitler which he knew existed among the Italian people. "*Hitler maledetto!*" (Hitler, the accursed!) he said in one of these messages. "Cut open the heart of an Italian killed in this war and you will find those two words there."

The seemingly tireless Fiorello was endangering his health by working too hard. When his doctor ordered him to stay home for a few days, he refused, saying, "This war is going to be won or lost in the harbor of New York." In any event he wasn't going to be in bed when it happened. Instead, he kept an appointment to pose for artists of the Society of Illustrators and Cartoonists. They had chosen him as their subject for a poster campaign to cut down absences by workers in war plants. His picture was to appear on the posters with the caption "Never-Take-a-Furlough-Fiorello."

While the cartoonists sketched away, he was interviewed by a lady reporter. She was overwhelmed by the list of his daily activities.

"Are you content with your work?" she asked.

"Right now I'd like to be in the army," he replied.

"But we need you here," the lady protested.

"That," the Mayor replied glumly, "is what the President says."

It was a verdict to which Fiorello could not reconcile himself.

CHAPTER 25

Washington Runaround

WHILE ROOSEVELT OCCUPIED THE WHITE HOUSE, LA Guardia continued to hope for a presidential appointment that would liberate him from civilian life. He had a number of private talks with FDR, but he refused to give any hint of what they were about.

When the news leaked out in the spring of 1943 that Fiorello might be appointed Civil Administrator of recaptured Italian territory in North Africa, he was cagey with the reporters. "I am still working on the budget of 1943-44 and not making any statements," he told them.

Nevertheless, *The New York Times* was able to report that the Mayor, expecting to be made a Brigadier General, had already selected associates to serve with him abroad. One of these assistants, said the news story, was to be Albert Spalding, the Italian-speaking violinist who had served with him in 1917. The story lacked only the detail that Chich Giordano was also preparing for the trip.

The Little Flower wrote to his friend, Harry Hopkins, in Washington:

"I saw the Chief yesterday—and I am so happy that I can be of service to my country—besides cleaning the streets of New York City. I expect to get my medical exam next week. The Chief indicated I could be commissioned . . . early in April.

"I am to be assigned to General Eisenhower's staff and I am convinced that I will be able to do a good job and be really useful . . .

"P.S. Writing this by hand as I do not want office to know until the last minute."

April came. The last handstitching was completed on his general's uniform. The Nazis were being pushed steadily westward by the Russians. Berlin was taking heavy punishment from English and Canadian bombers. The Japanese were on the defensive in Southeast Asia. And still no appointment for Fiorello. It became clear that there would not be one. Senator Harry S. Truman voiced his objection. Almost immediately afterward, Secretary of War Stimson called in the press to offer a polite but unconvincing explanation of why La Guardia would not be appointed:

"Mayor La Guardia visited me last Tuesday to offer personally and patriotically his services to the War Department. It was my view that in his present office as Mayor of New York, he is rendering direct to that city, and indirectly to the entire nation, an example of such usefulness that it is very difficult now to find any place in the Army in which he could be equally useful."

Even the most unfriendly of the newspapermen were pained by Stimson's humiliation of Fiorello. An editorial writer rushed to his defense the next day:

"The Mayor does not have to establish his physical courage. He did that in the last war. He does not have to establish his moral courage. He has been proving that ever since the last war."

Seniors at City College voted La Guardia the outstanding living New Yorker, but he would gladly have traded that compliment for a Brigadier's star. This public rejection was one of the deepest wounds in his lifetime, but he pretended to shrug it off.

"I've got a uniform of my own in New York, a street cleaning uniform," he quipped after Stimson's statement was published. "That's my own little army."

Taking into account the total number of city employees, the

Little Flower commanded quite a big army of almost 150,000—policemen, firemen, schoolteachers, office workers, mechanics, engineers, lawyers, truck drivers, magistrates, hospital workers—a long catalogue of skills, professions, and specialties.

It was an increasingly unmanageable army. To begin with, the Mayor had lost some of the best men on his team. Welfare Commissioner Hodson was killed in a plane crash. Health Commissioner Rice resigned because of illness. The fiery Fiorello, moreover, had quarreled with men like his personal aide, Clendenin Ryan; Tenement Commissioner Langdon Post, Civil Service Commissioner Paul Kern; Commissioner of Markets William Fellowes Morgan, Jr.; and Stanley Isaacs, Borough President of Manhattan for La Guardia's second term. Others, like A. A. Berle, Rexford Tugwell, Corporation Counsel Paul Windels, left New York to work in the national administration or to pursue better-paying private careers.

There were some sixteen thousand city employees on military leave. Replacements were hard to find. Those who stayed on their jobs complained that the cost of living rose faster than their pay. Fiorello was smarting under the public criticism of the schoolteachers, who said he interfered too much in education matters. Early in his administration, the Mayor had removed politics from the school system and restored much needed morale to the teaching profession. After he took office, appointments and promotions were made on the basis of professional merit instead of party influence. Toward the end of his third term, however, he became embroiled with the Board of Education in a struggle to exercise control over its authority and its policies. In the course of this conflict, a great many teachers developed the opinion that the Mayor was offering them too much advice and too little money.

Ordinary citizens with newly earned money in their pockets called him a kill-joy and a blue-nose, because he stopped bingo in movie theatres, cracked down on horse-race betting, and ran the burlesque shows out of town.

His relations with the newspapers got worse rather than better, but he used his Sunday radio talks to get back at his critics.

In one broadcast, he charged that the negligent attitude of the city's teachers was contributing to the sharp rise of wartime juvenile delinquency.

"Teachers say I am interfering with their work," he stormed, "but I think the schools would do well to devote a little extra time to teaching manners and respect for elders. Girls and boys should be taught to shine their shoes every day before going to school." And as a tactful gesture to his radio audience, he added, "Are you listening, Eric and Jean?"

What was the reason for the growing disenchantment between New York City and the greatest mayor it had ever had?

The common need that had held them together for the first ten years was losing its urgency. Fiorello's fighting dedication to a New Deal program for New Yorkers had made him a municipal hero. Now that there was a war on and jobs were available and saving money was a possibility, municipal affairs were less important to them than a decade earlier.

In Washington, the New Deal had been sidetracked under pressure from the wartime Congress which was at swords' points with the President. Though it supported him in all military matters, it opposed him at home in almost every bill that had any liberal intention. In his State of the Union message of January, 1944, FDR set forth an "Economic Bill of Rights" which would guarantee to all Americans the right to a decent living and a good education. Congress treated his pronouncement with silence. It ignored his reminder that "for two long years I have pleaded with Congress to take undue profits out of war."

It overrode his veto of a tax bill which, he thought, would allow excessive war profits to the big industries. He called it "not a tax bill but a tax *relief* bill providing relief not for the needy but for the greedy." The legislators denounced his statement as an insult.

As the year wore on, Fiorello was increasingly oppressed by a feeling of political aimlessness. The war had to be won, of course. But what would happen afterward? He saw a disquieting omen in the death of Senator Norris, stouthearted Progressive of the 1920's and staunchest of New Dealers. Norris had fought by his side from 1929 to 1932 for the passage of the Norris-La

Guardia Anti-Injunction Act. In 1942, Norris had been defeated for re-election after ten years in the House and thirty years in the Senate.

In a Sunday broadcast following the Senator's death, Fiorello revealed, more fully than he had intended, how much he was grieved at the news. He paid tribute to the liberal lion of Nebraska in the presence of reporters, city officials, and radio technicians:

"I know he died an unhappy man. The life of an insurgent in American politics is an unhappy one. He draws opposition from both parties and sometimes from three or four. He is always exposed to attack."

A tightness in his throat made the Little Flower falter. His eyes brimmed over.

"Senator Norris took his defeat hard," he said in a voice that trembled and broke. "He had a right to take it hard. He didn't expect it. Like all independents in politics, I guess he will get his reward and his credit in history books."

The bystanders were embarrassed when they saw the Mayor grope for a handkerchief to wipe away the tears. It seemed to them that he wept not only because a respected colleague had died, but because he glimpsed the loneliness of a road he might have to travel in his own turn.

La Guardia now addressed himself directly to his wife who was listening to the broadcast at home. "I'm coming home early this afternoon, Marie. I don't think I can work much more to-day." He had not forgotten the microphone in front of him, but he was not ashamed to reveal his emotion to the listeners. They were *his* people. They would understand. He signed off, as always, with his cheery exclamation, "Patience and Fortitude!" He needed both.

By September, the Allied Forces were on the Italian mainland at the tip of the "boot" and were pushing north toward Rome. La Guardia continued his battle against Hitler in New York. He spoke to the Italian people:

"While we attack the Nazis wherever they may be in your country, you can destroy their goods, you can destroy their water supply, and set fire to their supply depots!"

In one liberated Italian town, the local hero was a factory worker who had been jailed because he used to listen to La Guardia's broadcasts.

It took nine months to wrest Rome from the Nazis. The task was accomplished on June 5, and FDR hailed the event with the grim words, "One down and two to go." The next day was D-Day, the day of the long awaited allied invasion of France, under the command of General Dwight D. Eisenhower. The people of the United States stopped work long enough to offer a prayer for the safety of the Allied forces. There was a rush of blood donors to prepare for the great cost in casualties which is the price of military victories.

In July, Roosevelt was nominated for a fourth time as the Democratic candidate. The convention named Senator Harry S. Truman as his running mate. Mayor La Guardia went to Chicago to address the first large rally for FDR and made a stirring appeal for an election campaign which would renew the New Deal. "Give Franklin D. Roosevelt a Senate and House of Representatives that will work with him," he pleaded. "To elect a president and not give him a House and Senate would be like sending an army to the front without ammunition."

The Mayor and Harold Ickes electioneered at Madison Square Garden with the help of such popular entertainers as Ethel Merman and Frank Sinatra. On election eve, there was a Roosevelt rally at the Lucky Corner in East Harlem. Fiorello and Vito Marcantonio renewed, once again, their comradeship in political battle. Senator Robert F. Wagner shared the platform with them.

"It's just like old times to be here tonight," the Mayor told the crowd which filled the wide street. Although he was sure that FDR would be re-elected, he now had little hope that the New Deal would be able to take up, after the war, where it had left off after Pearl Harbor. It would not be like old times at all.

CHAPTER 26

Unfinished Business

WHEN FRANKLIN D. ROOSEVELT BEGAN HIS FOURTH
term on January 20, 1945, the twilight of New Deal liberalism
was at hand. Most Americans hardly noticed. Their eyes were on
the anticipated victory in Europe and Asia.

Allied bombers were blasting Berlin. The matchbox cities
of Japan were flaring and burning out under the nightly raids of
the B-29's. The Russians were plodding, grim and relentless,
through East Prussia and Czechoslovakia, on their way to the
heart of Hitler's crumbling Reich.

The world events of February and March, April, and May,
crowded each other out of the front pages and the special news
broadcasts with increasing rapidity. Roosevelt, Churchill, and
Stalin met at Yalta in February. British and American troops
smashed through the Siegfried Line and crossed the Rhine in
March. Shiploads of food, clothing, medical supplies, were sent
on their way to liberated, lacerated Europe from UNRRA, the
newly formed United Nations Relief and Rehabilitation Administration.

On April 25, Russian and American troops met and em-
braced each other on the banks of the German river, Elbe. Six
thousand air miles away, in San Francisco, that same day, forty-
six nations began a month-long meeting to constitute themselves

as the United Nations. And on May 8—VE-Day! The surrender of Germany! The end of the war in Europe!

But first, on April 12, there was the moment of inconsolable sorrow, that lingered beneath the exultation of May. Franklin Roosevelt died in his cottage at Warm Springs. The nation mourned as it had mourned for no man since Lincoln. It was not merely a President, but a wise leader and a valiant friend who had been lost. When the news of her husband's death was brought to Eleanor Roosevelt in Washington, she said: "I am more sorry for the people of the country and the world than I am for us." Harry S. Truman was sworn in as President at 7:09 that evening, but the vacuum left by Roosevelt's death extended beyond the time and place of the Missourian's induction.

Fiorello gave voice to his personal and to the public grief in a special broadcast over Station WNYC. Visibly shaken, he said:

"Though our leader has died, his inspiration is with us. His leadership is with us. His ideals live. That pattern is so definite, we cannot escape it; we do not want to escape it. I call upon all New Yorkers to carry on."

It was advice which Fiorello found harder and harder to follow as the weeks went by. He was confronted now, for the third time, with the question of whether he should carry on as Mayor. The Republican leaders of the five New York City boroughs or counties had declared early in the year that they would not support him for re-election.

To make matters worse, he could not be sure of a solid vote from organized labor even though he could have the American Labor Party nomination for the asking. The right wing of the ALP had split away to form the Liberal Party. Sidney Hillman and Vito Marcantonio, leading policy makers of the ALP, were loyal to Fiorello. But the chief of the new Liberal Party, Alex Rose, decided that he could do without La Guardia.

The same issues of the newspapers that reported Fiorello's tribute to the departed President also published Samuel Seabury's announcement that he was launching a new fourth-term fusion movement. The Judge was convinced that if Fiorello's name could be placed on the ballot, the people would elect him in spite of the massed opposition of the major-party leaders.

A political reporter for *The New York Times,* believed otherwise, with reservations. "La Guardia will not get the Republican nomination and he cannot win without it," he wrote.

"He has lost much of the political support he had four years ago." But, the writer added, "He still has strength among the rank-and-file of the city voters. His political recuperative powers have been amazing in the past and they may be again."

Fiorello earnestly believed, with excellent reason, that the people of the city still wanted him as their mayor. He was too seasoned a politician, however, to ignore the tremendous odds he would have to face in another election contest. Like all shrewd and self-respecting champions, he preferred to retire undefeated. Nevertheless, he made short work of a lightweight aspirant for the Republican nomination who presumed to criticize his stormy behavior in office. "The time has come," said the candidate, "to elect a mayor who would restore an atmosphere of courtesy and dignity to City Hall." To which Fiorello snorted, "It's no better for the people to be sold down the river with hypocritical politeness." On Sunday, May 6, he took his weekly radio audience of two million listeners into his confidence concerning his decision about a fourth term.

"There isn't a single county chairman of either the Democratic or the Republican Party who is in favor of my administration," he said. "Now isn't that grand! There isn't a single district leader of the political machines who wants to see me reelected. There isn't a political clubhouse loafer who hasn't shouted his head off against my administration. There is the proof, my friends, that these twelve years have not been in vain. It is proof that the men and women I appointed were not for sale."

He paused, then continued: "I am not going to run for mayor this year." He did not think it was good, he explained, for the same man to remain in the same office too long. "If an individual is in executive office too long," he said, "he may become bossy, and they tell me I'm sort of inclined that way at times," which was probably the greatest understatement of his twelve years in City Hall.

Fiorello sincerely abhorred the opposite shortcoming: "I do

not want to become so calloused that I could not lose my temper
when I hear of graft and when I hear of crime and racketeering."

He went into his personal reasons for retiring, too: "I will be
sixty-three in December. I have worked very hard. What I would
like to do is go out and get some sunshine and a little rest. I want
to store up more energy and vitality and just keep it in reserve in
case I should have to come back into public service . . ."

"As I look back," Fiorello said, "I see a sense of great comfort—I think it was possible to step into a tradition of corruption
and inefficiency, a history of favoritism and pilfering, a system of
patronage, and to change all that; to demonstrate to every writer
of history in our country who became hopeless and felt that local
government could not be good—I proved that he was wrong.
Yes, my friends, you gave me a job and I did it. Now I ask you to
carry on with patience and fortitude."

Having made his decision, Fiorello turned back to the daily
grind of being mayor. After the German surrender on May 8, he
tried to get on with the never ending task of building that great
metropolis, New York. In August, the war in the Pacific was
brought to an end by the appalling nuclear destruction of Hiro-
shima and Nagasaki.

In July, La Guardia's labors were momentarily interrupted
by dramatic personal news. His sister, Gemma Gluck; her
daughter, Yolanda Denes; and her year-and-a-half-old grandson,
Richard Denes, had been found in Berlin following their re-
moval from the Nazi concentration camp at Ravensbrueck. The
entire family had been arrested a year earlier after a Nazi newspaper published an inflammatory article which indignantly asked:
"How can the Hungarians permit the sister of Mayor La Guardia,
Hitler's greatest enemy, to live in Budapest?"

All three had escaped the gas chambers and the cremation
ovens, where millions of humans were processed to death with
the calm, assembly-line efficiency of an automobile factory.
Oddly enough, they owed their lives to the fact that they were
relatives of Fiorello La Guardia, whom the Nazis hated so
heartily.

"You are hostages," the camp commandant at Ravensbrueck
informed Gemma. "You will be exchanged for some other pris-

oners." The treatment given to the three indicated that the Germans put a high trade-in value on them. Gemma, Yolanda, and Richard were transferred to a prison in Berlin. When the Russians entered the city, the three were set adrift by their frightened jailers to find food and shelter as best they could. After weeks of effort in the chaos that followed the German surrender, Gemma managed to get word to the U. S. Army headquarters that she was in the city.

Mother, daughter, and grandson were immediately overwhelmed by reporters. One of them arranged for a private conversation between Fiorello and his sister over a special radio telephone channel. The conversation, as Gemma recalled it in her book, *My Story*, went like this:

"Hello, Sister!"

"Oh, Fiorello, is it really you? I can't believe it."

"No time for sentiments. Tell me what you want me to do and I'll do it."

When Gemma said that she wanted to come to the United States, he replied, "All right, Sister, but you must have patience. Things can't be arranged so quickly, and you know you must wait for your daughter's turn in the immigration quota, for I won't make any exceptions."

Gemma, Yolanda, and little Richard waited for a year in Germany and for another year in Denmark. They arrived in the United States, having learned meanwhile that the husbands of both women had died in the Matthausen concentration camp. Herman Gluck had been beaten to death by a guard. Yolanda's husband had died of malnutrition.

No time for sentimentality, Fiorello had said to Gemma. That applied to brother as well as sister. La Guardia had no intention of coasting through the last months of his last term. What he wanted to leave behind him was not a desk top swept bare of routine paperwork but a stack of unfinished business—civic projects that the new mayor would have to finish whether he liked it or not.

Among these projects was the International Airport at Idlewild, which had been in its early planning and building stages since 1941. There were schools, colleges, hospitals, sewage disposal plants, parks, playgrounds, zoos, libraries, museums, streets, parkways, bridges, and low-rent apartment buildings to be constructed, renovated, or improved.

In the third and last edition of "New York Advancing," the Mayor's periodic book-size reports on his administration, he wrote:

"I dreaded the thought of men returning home to find that there were no jobs for them . . . if I could prevent it, this would not happen in New York . . . Today we have a Postwar Works Program whose estimated total cost is $1,270,000,000 . . . In addition we are ready with $120,000,000 of low-rent public housing . . ."

Three terms as mayor, the added strain of the war years, and his own relentless demands on himself as a public servant, had begun to take their toll on Fiorello's health. There was a Sunday morning when Frank Giordano, as he often did, brought his barber's tools to Gracie Mansion, the eighteenth-century house on the shore of the East River, which had become the official residence of New York's Mayors in 1942. It seemed to Chich that his old comrade was subdued, listless. As he set about cutting the Mayor's hair, Fiorello groaned and said, "Chich, I don't feel well." Nevertheless, he turned up for his noonday broadcast showing no sign of his morning weariness.

A newspaper deliverer's strike which was in progress had halted all newspaper distribution in the city. As a result, New Yorkers were entirely dependent on radio broadcasts for their news. Fiorello knew that newspapers were also a source of entertainment to many people. On his first Sunday broadcast during the strike, he read the comic strips out loud from the published but generally unobtainable newspapers. Newspapers in the rest of the nation reported his performance with sympathetic amusement. The movie newsreel companies asked him to do it again. Fiorello agreed because he enjoyed his own performance and the publicity it produced. The comic strip he chose to read for the newsreel men was *Dick Tracy*.

"I wouldn't miss the comics myself, for anything," he told his listeners. "And there's no reason why you should miss them because those delivery men won't listen to my good advice and settle the strike." Then he plunged into a vivid picture-by-picture description of the quarrel between two thieves before they were caught by Detective Dick Tracy. In his reading, Fiorello made an aside to Police Commissioner Valentine: "Dick Tracy's been a detective so long and he still has that slender form. Lou Valentine, why do *our* detectives get fat, I wonder?" And addressing himself again to his listeners: "Say children, what does it all mean? It means that dirty money never brings any luck. No, dirty money always brings sorrow and sadness and misery and disgrace." He meant every word of it, of course.

The nation still recalls the Mayor's performance with an affectionate chuckle. Many remember his remarks about dirty money. But there were a lot of politicians in New York who weren't listening that day.

CHAPTER 27

Twilight Descends

FOR TWELVE UNPRECEDENTED YEARS, CITY HALL WAS the headquarters of a remarkable kind of mayor. He had his faults, but he deeply believed in government of the people, by the people, for the people. With Fiorello out of the running in the November, 1945, election, the politicians could hardly wait for the New Year to turn over an old leaf. They wanted government of the people by the machine and for the machine.

Before retiring from his post, Fiorello was determined to fight a final rear-guard action against the famished politicos who would come back on January 1, he was certain, to refresh themselves at the public treasury.

This noble and foredoomed struggle centered around the person of Newbold Morris, President of the City Council during the last two of Fiorello's three terms. Morris, the aristocrat of colonial descent, and La Guardia, the immigrant's son, had been warm friends as well as political allies since the spring of 1933, when Adolph Berle had introduced them to each other. They were sometimes spoken of, Morris recalls, as "the Little Flower and the Mayflower."

Morris would have been the logical choice as Republican candidate for mayor if the party leaders were interested in continuing La Guardia's program. They weren't, of course, and neither were the Democrats.

After considering a number of alternatives, La Guardia and Morris formed an independent slate, with Morris as candidate for mayor under the very independent name of the No Deal Party. *The New York Times*, the *New York Post*, Judge Seabury, and a number of influential "good government" liberals, such as Rabbi Wise, supported Morris. La Guardia campaigned and planned his strategy with all the energy, shrewdness, and heart he would have put into a fight for his own re-election. He had breakfast meetings with Morris and his running mates every morning at the Yale Club. All to no avail.

When the votes were counted William O'Dwyer, whom Fiorello had defeated in 1941, but who had come back from the war a Brigadier General, was Mayor of New York by some 700,-000 votes.

On Sunday, December 30, Fiorello made his farewell radio address from City Hall in the presence of some seventy officials, friends, reporters. As he hitched his chair toward the microphone on his desk, it was obvious that he would continue to be every inch the Mayor until his final handshake with the incoming General O'Dwyer. Nevertheless, he wanted his good-bys to the people of New York to be tranquil and affectionate.

"It is the holiday spirit," he began, "and I am not going to say a great many things I wanted to say . . . we want to start the New Year happy and cheerful."

He did not hurl his favorite epithet, "tinhorns," at the bookmakers and other professional promoters of gambling. He reminded his listeners, lovingly, for the zillionth time, that most of the hundreds of millions of dollars bet on horse races in New York City were risked by people who couldn't afford to lose. He urged the horse-players: "Put two dollars on the wife, two on the oldest boy, and two on the little girl. I guarantee that you will win."

Though he was striving for sweetness and light in his last broadcast as mayor, nothing on earth could have prevented La Guardia from commenting that the City Council had voted down a forty-five-million-dollar appropriation for the new Idlewild Airport.

"I am going to appeal to him [Mayor O'Dwyer] again, about

the great mistake and the great damage to our city in scuttling
the Idlewild Airport," he said. "I would rather not tell the whole
story. It is not a nice story but if I have to, I will tell you about it
Sunday at twelve o'clock."

From a boy who signed himself "City Ruffian," Fiorello read
a letter saying, "I took a light out of one of your city parks. En-
closed is cost." There were eighteen-cents worth of postage
stamps attached. Fiorello commented, "No, son, you are not a
ruffian at all. You did the right thing in sending the eighteen
cents . . . and don't call yourself a little ruffian again. You are a
good boy." He also had some relatively mild comments to make
about loan sharks and black market deals in textiles. As his air
time ran out, he took leave of his listeners by reading them a
prayer written generations earlier by the Abolitionist clergyman,
Theodore Parker:

> . . . Give me the power to labor for mankind;
> Make me the mouth of such as cannot speak;
> Eyes let me be to groping men and blind,
> A conscience to the base; and to the weak
> Let me be hands and feet; and to the foolish, mind;
> And lead still further on, such as Thy Kingdom seek.

"And give me patience and fortitude," he added.

There was another moment of public farewell on New
Year's Day, when he gave official welcome to the newly inaugurated mayor. After posing with O'Dwyer for the photographers,
he walked out of the building with Marie. Before getting into
their modest Ford sedan at the curb, he took off his big black hat,
smiled broadly and waved up at City Hall. The newspaper photographers asked him to repeat the gesture. He did; then he went
into the car and drove off.

The day and the hour were a reminder to his listeners that
they would be able to go on hearing him, without skipping a
Sunday, on a new radio program over Station WJZ, sponsored by
a dairy company. And they did hear from him. In May, 1946, he
announced his plans to dictate memos, "I Am Telling You Now,"
warning the public against projects privately or publicly sponsored which he considered inconsistent with the public welfare:

"I will dictate them so that you can hear them now and then, and we will make a sound recording of them. I will deposit one in the Municipal Library, and two or three of them elsewhere, and when the time comes, in two, three, four, or maybe ten years from now, you can just pick them out and say, 'La Guardia told you so.' "

The whereabouts of "I Am Telling You Now" is a mystery today.

La Guardia had also contracted with *Liberty* magazine for a weekly coast-to-coast broadcast on national affairs over the American Broadcasting Company network. In addition, he started a weekly column, "Under the Hat," printed as an advertisement on behalf of a large chain of furniture stores in four New York newspapers, and he made his appearance as an editorial columnist in the liberal newspaper, *PM*. His headquarters for these activities, which required a staff of six secretaries, was an office on the fiftieth floor of the RCA Building in Rockefeller Plaza, which also housed the radio studios from which he did his broadcasting.

For Fiorello H. La Guardia, private citizen, the view from the fiftieth floor was no different than he had ever found it at soapbox level in East Harlem. In his new occupations as radio commentator and columnist, he still considered himself a spokesman for the ordinary man.

His furniture store column criticized the Federal Office of Price Administration for relaxing its control of food prices and called for the passage of a national Fair Employment Practices Law. In his *PM* column, he attacked the *New York Daily News* for what he considered to be its lax treatment of the truth. On his WJZ program for New York listeners, he urged the establishment of a permanent United Nations headquarters in New York City. On his coast-to-coast ABC program, he argued against Congressional proposals to eliminate funds for the Federal school lunch program, and at the same time, reduce taxes on whiskey and luxury goods. "As between whiskey and milk," he proclaimed, "I am for milk. As between the booze hounds and the children, I am for the children."

Fiorello was not destined to settle down to the role of hired

political pundit for sellers of mild cheese or strong furniture. Deprived of an important national role in the winning of the war,
he leaped at the chance to shoulder an international responsibility in the establishment of the peace. He was chosen by the
United Nations Relief and Rehabilitation Administration as its
Director General to replace New York State's former Governor
Herbert H. Lehman, who had resigned. He took the job without pay, as Lehman had done. The organization had been set up
in 1943 to feed the people and re-establish the industries of areas
liberated from the Fascist armies. Long before Fiorello's appointment in March, 1946, however, it had become a subject of controversy in Congress and in the newspapers.

The division of the world into Communist, anti-Communist,
and uncommitted nations had not yet become a hard fact. The
"cold war" had barely begun. There was sharp debate, however,
as to what our national policy toward the Soviet Union should
be in the future. Those who advocated a "get tough" policy with
Russia objected to UNRRA because it was not exclusively under
United States control. Considerable United Nations' help was
going to China, Czechoslovakia, Greece, Italy, Poland, the
Ukraine, and Yugoslavia. These countries were among the hard-
est hit by the war, but they were not responsive to American
leadership. There were many Americans who supported the then
respectable opinion that the success of our wartime alliance with
the Soviets could become the basis for peacetime co-operation.
They felt that UNRRA was a good way to begin. They wanted
the United States to work for the realization of the dream Franklin Roosevelt had expressed in a report to Congress six weeks
before his death:

". . . an end to the system of unilateral action and exclusive
alliances and spheres of influence and balances of power and all
the other expedients which have been tried for centuries—and
have failed."

They took to heart Roosevelt's admonition that as a nation
"we must cultivate the science of human relationships—the ability of all peoples, of all kinds, to live together and work together,
in the same world, at peace."

Fiorello La Guardia, who had accomplished the remarkable

feat of running a nonpartisan city for twelve years, could not resist the idea of a nonpartisan world. Feeding hungry people who
had no means of feeding themselves had been a familiar and end-
lessly gratifying task to him. Doing the same thing on a global
scale was his idea of a job worth all the effort he could expend. If
people were hungry, he was going to feed them, and he didn't
care if they liked Joseph Stalin or Winston Churchill. He said
as much before he accepted the appointment:

"It is food that is needed. People are crying for bread not for
advice . . . In our country they have learned through a period
of depression that ticker tape ain't spaghetti." He warned that he
would insist on "fast-moving ships loaded with food to fight fam-
ine, and not slow-moving resolutions to please politicians."

To the people who propagandized against UNRRA, and
sneered at the organization as a "world-wide WPA" and a "global
boondoggle," Fiorello replied that if there were no UNRRA
there would be a world-wide Tammany instead. Food and financial help to needy nations would become an instrument in the
game of power politics. "And," he declared before the United
Nations, "the world has had war after war because of power politics."

During Fiorello's last year as mayor, Newbold Morris and
other of his close associates saw signs that the Little Flower's
health was not what it should be. When reporters asked Fiorello
how he felt, he usually answered, "Fine," because he had a strong
man's distaste for talking about his weaknesses. Anyway, there is
no other answer a man in public office can give. Yet, the
UNRRA job seemed to revitalize him. In the face of the discour-
aging facts that had driven ex-Governor Lehman from the post
of UNRRA Director, Fiorello pictured his mission as one of
history's great humanitarian crusades.

"It is all so hopeful," he said, "as never before in the whole
history of the world—forty-eight nations coming together to
save lives. We are united to preserve life, to build, not to kill, not
to destroy. There is precedent for it in the old Scripture and in
the new Scripture—to love our neighbor, to aid the needy. That
is not original. It just hasn't been carried on. As the sun rises from
place to place, in every language spoken by man—'give us this

day our daily bread'—that is all there is to it, to respond to that prayer. We then become a great army of mercy. That is the mission of UNRRA, and that is the army I am going to lead."

It was a scattered and disorganized army. His efforts at leadership took him half way around the world on trips of inspection and negotiation with heads of state in Germany, Italy, Austria, Yugoslavia, Poland, Russia, Greece, Egypt. His months of wearying air travel between April and the end of the year permitted him, or perhaps compelled him, to renew his comradeship with Frank Giordano somewhat after the fashion of their days at the Foggia aviation base. Chich became the Sergeant again to his belligerent little bulldog of a Major. It was apparent that Fiorello needed to be looked after. Affectionately, discreetly, Chich made sure that Fiorello was properly fed, rested, and attired.

Officially, Fiorello remained Director General of UNRRA until the end of 1946, when it was disbanded and its work was handed over to other United Nations agencies. His activity for the organization began to taper off in the fall.

Early in September, a day before he returned to the United States, Fiorello addressed a conference of the UN Food and Agricultural Organization at Copenhagen, and managed to trample heavily on the toes of some internationally important business interests. He warned that the world must "discard the system in which one country has an abundance and another country is in need. It is no use saying," he stormed, "that we are not going to interfere with free exchange and free sales. If you do what is needed, you *will* interfere and will put every dabbling grain exchange out of business in Chicago, Winnipeg, Liverpool, or wherever it exists."

It was one thing for Fiorello to call New York gamblers "tinhorns" but it was quite another for him to hint that traders on the world's grain exchanges were gamblers. On his return to New York the following day, he found himself under attack by the Chicago Board of Trade, which deemed his speech "scurrilous and perhaps libelous." He was accused of "fostering a plan which calls for socializing the production and marketing of wheat and thereby scrapping the most efficient method of doing business that has ever been evolved."

Fiorello shrugged his shoulders and went about his work. To reporters who asked him what kind of work that would be, he replied, "minding other people's business."

Under this heading, he appeared before a Congressional committee to protest against the lifting of Federal controls on food prices and rent. Calling himself a "representative of unorganized Americans," he advocated a strong Federal housing program, a national health insurance bill, and a guaranteed annual wage for most categories of workers. He was indignant at Congressional proposals for new laws which would, in effect, wipe out much of the protection enjoyed by trade unions under the Wagner Labor Act which was an important foundation stone of the New Deal. Such bills, he charged, were the product of angry special interests rather than genuine national necessity.

"I was never frightened about the outcome of the war, frightful as I knew it must be," he said. "It was always the post-war period which frightened me."

Though Fiorello sensed that his retirement from public office was final, the mere sight of the city could console him. There was almost no place he could look without being aware of some constructive mark of his mayoralty. His effort and his ability, his shrewdness, anger and love, his dedication to the people were cemented into the bricks and the sidewalks of New York. He had worked not only to enlarge the city's possessions but to provide more elbow room for the human spirit.

During the New Deal years he had been a warm champion of the concerts, paintings, theatre performances, and literary undertakings of the Federal Arts Projects in New York. And World War II had not deterred him from realizing, to some extent, his own private dream of culture for the masses at popular prices. In 1943, he had used his authority as mayor to establish the New York City Center of Music and Drama. Two decades later it was still a flourishing institution which offered drama, opera, ballet, and musical performances of the highest merit.

The comfort Fiorello took from the inner knowledge that he had fought boldly and triumphed splendidly for the people of his city was mixed with uneasiness. In his "Mayor's Final Report," in the last edition of "New York Advancing," he had written:

"The City is ready again with a gigantic public works program. I leave the blue prints and plans and specifications, every detail ready, to my successors . . . All that is necessary—pull out the plans and go to work. Don't mess it up, I beg of my successor. It is so easy to mess it up . . . Graft has been eliminated. It would be so easy for it to creep back again. Don't let that happen . . ."

Well, it was out of Fiorello's hands now, but those whose lives had been touched by his would know that he had worked hard and achieved much on their behalf. Along with many allies, he made his contribution toward altering the concept of government to meet conditions of the twentieth century. Unemployment insurance, disability payments, and retirement pensions for the aged had become facts of life in his day.

La Guardia's contribution toward progress was massive. Throughout his public career he had held political office not to enrich himself but to better the lot of his constituents.

He was honored, somewhat grudgingly at home, perhaps, but unstintingly abroad. He became an honorary citizen of Foggia, where his father was born and where he had flown against the enemies of Italy. A plaque marked the house where he had lived in Fiume. There were La Guardia schools, hospitals, and streets scattered through Europe and there was even an *S.S. La Guardia* which docked at Naples before making its maiden voyage across the Atlantic.

In May, 1947, he was made the year's recipient of the One World Award established by the Wendell Willkie Memorial. The accolade, which included a flight around the world, was conferred on Fiorello in Carnegie Hall before an overflow audience of representatives of some thirty national groups in New York City's population. In his speech of acknowledgment, La Guardia said, "I don't think I can take that wonderful trip. I'm too busy and my health is not as good as it should be."

During April, painful illness had forced him into Mt. Sinai Hospital, barely a block away from the apartment building where he had lived during most of his years as mayor. His doctors allowed him to go out to keep important engagements. They knew he was stricken, incurably, with cancer and they were helping him borrow time.

In mid-June, more desperately than hopefully, they resorted to surgery. When Fiorello recovered from the operation, he went back to his house in Riverdale, in the Bronx, to work—to think, to write, to mind other people's business—as well and as long as his ebbing life would permit. It never occurred to him to give up.

Some of his friends who were prominent in public life undertook to substitute for him on his weekly WJZ broadcasts—Judge Seabury, Adolph Berle, Rabbi Wise, Newbold Morris, and others. To the best of his ability, Fiorello tried to maintain editorial authority over their contributions. After hearing a radio talk which Newbold Morris had delivered, he exclaimed, "No, no, Newbold! Put more hell into it."

Robert Moses, Fiorello's old Park Commissioner, superadministrator and intermittent thorn-in-the-side, recalls that "when the Mayor sent for me late in the summer of 1947, I was shocked at the change in him. He was in bed, so shrunken, so chap-fallen, and yet so spunky and so obviously on his way out, I felt like crying. It was a battle that not even the most courageous fighter could win."

Chich was with Fiorello when he died. Almost at the very end the Little Flower told Chich, "I've got to live . . . the people need me."

At 8:06 on the morning of September 20, 1947, the 5-5-5-5 bell, repeated four times, sounded on the signal system of the New York City Fire Department. It was the traditional announcement of mourning which marks the death of a fireman in the line of duty or the passing of an important city official. In this case it tolled the death of Fiorello H. La Guardia, in his sixty-fourth year.

Mayor O'Dwyer proclaimed a day of mourning. At Flushing Meadows, in the hall of the General Assembly, representatives of fifty-five nations stood in silent tribute.

In the chapel at the Cathedral of St. John the Divine, Fiorello lay in state. On the Saturday of his death and the day that followed, some 45,000 New Yorkers walked by his bier in a slow reverent line. Some paused only for a sorrowful farewell look. Others crossed themselves or stood still to pray. A woman dropped a rose into the coffin saying, "Poor Mayor La Guardia, he's gone." A man said, "He helped us all." To *The New York Times* reporter who looked on as the plain people said a last farewell to their three-time Mayor, "the demonstration of respect and affection was one of the greatest in the history of the city."

Of the 9,500 who attended the funeral services on Monday morning, 8,500 were ordinary folks. Only one thousand seats had been reserved for city, state, and national officials, for diplomats of the UNRRA nations and UN members, and for close personal friends.

The funeral procession, some forty automobiles, made its way across Harlem and the Bronx, to Woodlawn Cemetery, past silent crowds lining the curbstones.

Marie, Gemma, and Chich Giordano rode together in the black limousine behind the hearse. At Woodlawn, when the last obsequies were performed and the coffin was lowered into the earth, Chich, red-eyed and shaken, did what he could to comfort his beloved comrade's wife and sister. But who was there to comfort him? Chich was one of New York's millions of little people. He had just assisted in the burial of the man who spoke for him and fought for him. He would have to wait for the coming of another champion.

Bibliography

Allen, Frederick Lewis, *Only Yesterday*. New York, Harper & Brothers, 1931.

Allen, William H., *Why Tammanys Revive: La Guardia's Mis-Guard*. New York, Institute for Public Service, 1937.

Beard, Charles A., and Mary R., *The Rise of American Civilization*. New York, The MacMillan Company, 1930.

Boyer, Richard O., and Morais, Herbert, M., *Labor's Untold Story*. New York, Cameron Associates, 1955.

Brandt, Lillian, *An Impressionist View of the Winter of 1930-31*. New York, National Welfare Council, 1932.

Browne, Carl, *When Coxey's "army" marcht on Washington* [sic], *1894*.

Collman, Charles Albert, *Our Mysterious Panics*. New York, William Morrow & Co., 1931.

Commager, Henry Steele, *The Story of the Second World War*. Boston, Little Brown & Co., 1945.

Cuneo, Ernest, *Life with Fiorello*. New York, The MacMillan Company, 1955.

Federal Writers' Project of the Works Progress Administration, *Arizona, The Grand Canyon State*, revised edition. New York, Hastings House, 1956.

Federal Writers' Project of the Works Progress Administration, *New York City Guide*. New York, Random House, 1939.

Fowler, Gene, *Beau James: The Life of Jimmy Walker*. New York, The Viking Press, 1949.

Franklin, Jay, *La Guardia: A Biography*. New York, Modern Age Books, 1937.

Gluck, Gemma La Guardia, *My Story*. New York, David McKay Co., 1961.

Ickes, Harold L., *The Secret Diary of Harold L. Ickes: The First Thousand Days* (*1933-1936*). New York, Simon and Schuster, 1953.

Ickes, Harold L., *The Struggle Inside* (*1936-1939*). New York, Simon and Schuster, 1953.

Keithley, Ralph, *Buckey O'Neill.* Caldwell, Idaho, The Caxton Print-
ers, Ltd., 1949.

Labor Research Association, *The Making of an Insurgent: An Autobiography (1882-1919).* Philadelphia, J. B. Lippincott Company,
1948.

Limpus, Lowell W., and Leyson, Burr W., *This Man La Guardia.*
New York, E. P. Dutton & Co., 1938.

McMurray, Donald L., *Coxey's Army.* Boston, Little, Brown & Co.,
1929.

Mann, Arthur, *La Guardia, A Fighter Against His Times, 1882-1933.*
Philadelphia, J. B. Lippincott Company, 1959.

Martin, Michael, and Gelber, Leonard, *Dictionary of American History.* Paterson, New Jersey, Littlefield Adams & Co., 1959.

Mitchell, Broadus, *Depression Decade: From New Era Through New
Deal, 1929-1941.* New York, Rinehart and Company, 1947.

Moley, Raymond, *27 Masters of Politics.* New York, Funk & Wag-
nalls Co., 1949.

Morris, Newbold, *Let the Chips Fall.* New York, Appleton-Century-
Crofts, 1955.

Moscow, Warren, *Politics in the Empire State.* New York, Alfred A.
Knopf, 1948.

Moses, Robert, *La Guardia: A Salute and a Memoir.* New York,
Simon and Schuster, 1957.

Rankin, Rebecca B., ed., *Guide to Municipal Government: City of
New York,* fifth edition. New York, The Eagle Library, Inc., 1942.

Rankin, Rebecca B., ed., *New York Advancing: Victory Edition,
Seven More Years of Progressive Administration in the City of
New York, 1939-1945.* New York, Municipal Reference Library,
1945.

Rochester, Anna, *The Populist Movement in the United States.* New
York, International Publishers Co., 1943.

Rubenstein, Annette T., ed., *I Vote My Conscience: Debates,
Speeches and Writings of Vito Marcantonio.* New York, Marcantonio Memorial, 1956.

Sayre, Wallace S., and Kaufman, Herbert, *Governing New York
City: Politics in the Metropolis.* New York, Russell Sage Foundation, 1960.

Schlesinger, Arthur M., Jr., *The Age of Roosevelt,* Vol I: *The Crisis
of the Old Order.* Boston, Houghton Mifflin Company, 1957.

Shannon, David A., *The Great Depression.* New York, Prentice-Hall,
1960.

Sherwood, Robert E., *Roosevelt and Hopkins: An Intimate History.*
New York, Harper & Brothers, 1948.

Spalding, Albert, *Rise to Follow: An Autobiography.* New York,
Henry Holt & Co., 1943.

Thomas, Norman, and Blanshard, Paul, *What Is the Matter with New York*. New York, The MacMillan Company, 1931.

Tucker, Ray, and Barkley, Frederick R., *Sons of the Wild Jackass*. New York, L. C. Page & Company, 1932.

Tugwell, Rexford Guy, *The Democratic Roosevelt*. New York, Doubleday & Company, 1957.

Tugwell, Rexford Guy, *The Art of Politics*. New York, Doubleday & Company, 1958.

Valentine, Lewis J., *Night Stick*. New York, New York Dial Press, 1947.

Warren, Harris Gaylord, *Herbert Hoover and the Great Depression*. New York, Oxford University Press, 1959.

Werner, R. M., *Tammany Hall*. New York, Doubleday, Doran & Co., 1928.

Wilson, Edmund, *The American Earthquake*. New York, Doubleday & Company, 1958.

Documents, collections, newspapers, and periodicals consulted include the following main sources.

Columbia University: Oral History Research Office, *Reminiscences of Stanley M. Isaacs*. 1950. *Reminiscences of Marie La Guardia*. 1950.

Columbia University Library: Kilroe Collection of Tammany Material.

Columbia University School of Journalism Library, Library Morgue.

Municipal Archives and Records of New York City.

Municipal Reference Library.

New York School of Social Work Library.

New York Public Library: American History Collection; newspaper files of *The New York Times;* periodicals; the Congressional Record.

Index